An Educator's Journey To Improve Chemistry Instruction

Reflective Practice and Learning Theory

An Educator's Journey To Improve Chemistry Instruction

Reflective Practice and Learning Theory

Dr. Jason Solomon

EXCELLER BOOKS®
A GLOBAL PRESS

An Educator's Journey to Improve Chemistry Instruction
Reflective Practice and Learning Theory

Cover by Exceller Books

ISBN: 978-93-47397-76-9

Published in India in 2026 by Exceller Books,
An imprint of GE Group,
G1, Dream Apartment, Degree College Road, Belgharia,
Kolkata, 700056, India
www.excellerbooks.com

EXCELLER BOOKS®
A GLOBAL PRESS

Acknowledgement

I would first like to acknowledge God, the father and Jesus Christ. Jesus has been a constant source of strength, protection, and inspiration. I am assured that I am never alone and that someone truly values my well-being. My family has been a significant source of motivation, especially my father, Uriah Solomon, and my deceased mother, Sherron Williams. They expect me to do my best and never stop striving to make something meaningful of my life. For instance, being a decent classroom teacher during my lifetime would make them proud. It does not matter whether I become a school principal, an education officer, or obtain a high-level position. They just want to know that their son did something meaningful with his life. A big thank you goes to Dr. Edward Lambert, my academic advisor and Amiakhor Ejaeta, my tutor, for their guidance and support throughout the program.

Overview

This study addresses persistent challenges in the teaching and learning of Caribbean Secondary Education Certificate (CSEC) Chemistry, including low student engagement, difficulty mastering abstract concepts, and teachers' struggles with completing the syllabus. The purpose was to evaluate classroom materials already used in teaching to identify instructional strengths and weaknesses, align practices with learning theories and learning styles, and propose targeted improvements.

A reflective-practitioner inquiry approach was applied, combining document analysis of lesson plans, assessments, classroom evaluations, and teacher reflections. Data were examined for alignment with pedagogical best practices, and improvements were developed using constructivism, cognitive load theory, experiential learning, and social constructivism, alongside visual, auditory, and kinesthetic learning styles. The analysis revealed that existing materials showed strengths in promoting practical engagement, incorporating real-world applications, and fostering collaborative learning. However, weaknesses included insufficient scaffolding for complex concepts, limited differentiation for diverse learner needs, and inconsistent integration of technology. Suggested improvements focused on restructuring lesson sequences for clearer concept progression, embedding more formative assessment opportunities, expanding inclusive teaching strategies, and enhancing the use of digital tools to support visualization and experimentation.

Based on the literature review, a framework of 11 components of chemistry education was proposed as a basis for researching, evaluating, and enhancing instruction. These components, presented as new knowledge, serve as a guide for building a more inclusive, engaging, and conceptually sound chemistry education framework. The analysis also underscored the value of behavior management strategies, such as clear rules, active supervision, and proactive engagement, in fostering a positive, productive learning environment.

The proposed resource offers teachers adaptable, evidence-based strategies to enhance lesson delivery and student understanding. For researchers, it provides a structured framework for examining chemistry education through reflective practice. For society, it promotes scientific literacy and problem-solving skills essential for addressing real-world challenges. While the improvements have yet to be widely implemented, they present a scalable, theory-informed model for strengthening chemistry education in the Caribbean and beyond.

Table of Contents

Introduction

"Education is the most powerful weapon which you can use to change the world." – Nelson Mandela

The book introduces the history of education, science, and chemistry education, focusing on challenges in student engagement and content retention in chemistry education. It highlights the disconnect between educational theory and classroom practice, aiming to improve instructional design through reflective inquiry and classroom analysis. The research will evaluate teaching strengths and weaknesses, learning theories, and how classroom evaluations can enhance practice in Caribbean Secondary Education Certificate (CSEC) chemistry education.

History of Education

The history of education is reflected in the history of reform movements and ideas (Oye, 2001). This is evident from Plato's *Politeia*, where education is considered a force or the foundation for changing culture, society, and even individuals. For instance, education was regarded as the voice of God during the late Roman Empire and early Christian period. Basically, God's will was reflected in education.

Religion has deeply influenced education throughout history. During the medieval period, religious institutions controlled much of the education system, often shaping curricula to reflect religious teachings. For example, monks and priests were responsible for preserving knowledge and teaching basic literacy through the Bible and religious texts. The Reformation, beginning in the 16th century, also transformed education, with figures like Martin Luther pushing for universal education so that all Christians could read the Bible for themselves (Oye, 2001).

Key Events in the Development of Education:

1. The invention of writing (c. 3000 BCE) – Writing enabled the recording and transmission of knowledge, marking the birth of formal education systems. *Example:* The Sumerians developed cuneiform, one of the earliest systems of writing, which played a crucial role in organizing early education (Robinson, 2002).
2. Medieval guilds (c. 1100–1500 CE) – Guilds functioned as early vocational institutions, training individuals in specialized trades. *Example:* The apprenticeship system in medieval guilds provided the foundation for modern vocational education (De Vries, 2002).
3. Medieval free cities (c. 12th century) – Free cities fostered an environment for educational growth, especially in urban areas. *Example:* The establishment of the University of Paris in the 12th century became a model for education in European cities (Berman, 1983).
4. The establishment of universities (c. 12th–13th century) – The rise of universities provided a platform for higher education, particularly in the fields of law, medicine, and theology. *Example:* The University of Bologna, established in 1088, is widely regarded as the first university in Europe (Cavallo, 2001).
5. The Reformation (1517) – The Reformation introduced educational reforms, particularly with an emphasis on literacy and Bible translation. *Example:* Martin Luther's Bible translation highlighted the need for education to foster personal interpretation of religious texts (Snyder, 2009).
6. Colonialism (16th–20th century) – Colonial powers introduced education systems designed to control and "civilize" local populations. *Example:* The British colonization of India saw the establishment of English-

language schools to serve their colonial interests (Banerjee, 2004).

7. The New England War on Satan (1670s) – This event highlighted the role of education in religious moral control. *Example:* The Massachusetts Bay Colony passed laws in 1647 requiring literacy in order to read the Bible (Kramer, 2015).
8. The failure of New Hampshire State College (early 19th century) – Some early educational institutions in the U.S. struggled with financial instability. *Example:* The closure of New Hampshire State College led to the rise of public libraries, as communities sought alternative ways to provide access to education and knowledge (Field, 2016).
9. Female teachers entering the classroom (mid-19th century) – The rise of female teachers led to a transformation in educational practices, especially in primary education. *Example:* By the mid-19th century, women represented the majority of teachers in American schools (Litt, 2007).
10. World War I (1914–1918) – World War I led to reforms in education systems, with a focus on fostering unity and preparing citizens for post-war life. *Example:* After the war, many countries expanded their public education systems to address the needs of a rapidly changing society (Green, 2003).
11. Religious monasteries and schools (5th–15th century) – Monasteries were centers of learning, preserving ancient texts and advancing education in medieval Europe. *Example:* Benedictine monks played a key role in educational developments through monastic schools (Tierney, 2013).
12. Horace Mann's reforms (1837) – Horace Mann, a key figure in the development of public education in the United States, advocated free and universal education. *Example:* Mann's reforms in Massachusetts were instrumental in shaping the modern public school system (Katz, 1987).

Education is diverse, spanning many areas such as religion, arts, mathematics, literature and language, and science. Science education will be emphasized to explore its history.

History of Science Education

Science education is the process of equipping learners with scientific skills, encouraging curiosity, and fostering a positive attitude towards science. Science education allows learners to gain an understanding of the natural world and to interact with technology and science within society (European Science before the Year 1600, n.d.). For instance, in Europe before the year 1600, science was a mix of religion, astrology, alchemy, and some other scientific disciplines. Classical works by Greek and Roman authors were the gold standard of mathematics and science literature. Prominent authors of that time were Aristotle, Euclid, and Pliny. The invention of the printing press led to a demand for those authors' works.

"Where the conflict really lies," wrote Alvin Plantinga in his book, highlighting the long-standing relationship between science and religion (Davis, 2022). Both science and religion explain that we live in a world that is ordered and structured, and that attaining knowledge gives a greater understanding. Many important figures at the foundation of science have strong ties to religion. For example, John Sacrobosco, who was a medieval mathematician and astronomer, was also a clergyman. Also, René Descartes, Robert Boyle, and Isaac Newton were devoted Christians. The atomic theory, one of the most fundamental and important concepts in science education, was developed by John Dalton, a Quaker. The individuals mentioned contributed to the development of science through their research and books. In earlier periods, such as the medieval period in Europe, monasteries were centers that preserved knowledge, and the monks acted as educators (Jackson, 1992).

During the 18th and 19th centuries, science education began to take a formal shape in schools. With the advancement of industrial society, there was a growing need for individuals trained in scientific thinking and problem-solving. This led to the inclusion of science in formal school curricula across Europe and North America. Institutions such as the Royal Society in England and various French academies played a role in shaping structured science instruction. Over time, disciplines like physics, chemistry, and biology became core subjects in secondary education. These changes laid the groundwork for how science is taught in the modern classroom (DeBoer, 1991).

Also, the scientific revolution helped to advance the development of science education. The revolution encompassed the period between Copernicus and Newton (Renn & Damerow, 2015). It stemmed from Aristotelian natural philosophy, backed by church authority, leading to the classical sciences and their institutions, as seen between 1500 and 1700. There was a challenge to traditional natural philosophy in offering explanations for natural phenomena and in seeing science as an avenue to attain mastery over nature. The scientific revolution led to the rise of heliocentric astronomy and classical mechanics and contributed to fields such as optics, chemistry, and physiology. These advancements resulted in numerous technological breakthroughs (Renn & Damerow, 2015).

History of Chemistry Education

The rise of chemistry education can trace its roots to ancient times through herbal medicine, alchemy, and metallurgy. People used herbs to treat illness and passed down their knowledge by word of mouth. Alchemy and metalwork also helped people understand how substances change, even if they did not know the science behind it.

Ancient Foundations

The roots of alchemy can be traced to Alexandria, the heart of Hellenistic Egypt, and its theoretical foundation is grounded in Aristotelian philosophy (Coyne, 2023). The practice of alchemy was brought to medieval Europe by Arabic scholars. The main goals of alchemy were to transform other metals into gold and to create a philosopher's stone. The philosopher's stone was believed to grant eternal youth if successfully created. Additionally, alchemy was applied in many practical areas, such as metallurgy and dye-making. Although often viewed as sorcery, alchemy is now recognized as a foundational stage in the development of modern chemistry. This perception did not prevent prominent scientists from drawing upon alchemical knowledge. For instance, Robert Boyle, who is considered the father of chemistry, advocated for experimentation and empirical observation, which are the foundations of the scientific method, and he is thought to have been influenced by alchemical ideas. In fact, Boyle was accused of borrowing significantly from alchemy in the development of his corpuscular theory. Another important figure in science, Isaac Newton, had a vast collection of alchemical writings, linking his work to alchemical thought. Newton's law of universal gravitation is believed to have been inspired, in part, by alchemical concepts (Coyne, 2023). This highlights that alchemy was not just mad men playing with chemicals and various substances, but a legitimate science.

Figure 1.1: An Artistic Representation of Alchemy

How Did the Alchemy Knowledge Survive?

In ancient times, knowledge was passed from person to person, such as from one family member to another or from a master to a student. This means that apprenticeship was one method used to pass on skills such as metallurgy, dyeing, and medicine. Apprenticeship is defined as a form of training in which an individual learns an art, trade, or craft from someone having expert knowledge in that area. Apprenticeship evolved into more complex forms, as an apprentice (trainee) and a master (trainer) established a legal contract stipulating the duration and conditions of the apprentice-master relationship (Nielsen, 2010). For example, a formal European apprenticeship involving guilds had written contracts signed by master and apprentice, which were usually valid for a four-year period. At the end of the period, the apprentice was tested and accredited as a journeyman of the trade (Nielsen, 2010). Ancient knowledge, such as alchemy, was not only preserved through apprenticeship and oral tradition but also through texts.

The *Emerald Tablet* is one of the most important historical texts on alchemy. It was translated from an Arabic text into Latin (Amr & Tbakhi, 2007). The text reflects knowledge relating to Hellenistic, Christian, and Islamic traditions. In the Arabic version, a Christian invocation and priestly figure can be found. The *Emerald Tablet* shows its alchemical roots by mentioning classical representations of elements used in alchemy: fire (sun), water (moon), air (wind), and earth. The work of alchemy can be seen more academically in the works of Jabir ibn Hayyan. Abu Musa Jabir Ibn Hayyan Al-Azdi is considered the father of Arab chemistry and one of the founders of modern pharmacy. He is known as the European Geber and was born in the city of Tus in the province of Khorasan in Iran in 721 AD. He knew chemistry (alchemy), pharmacy, philosophy, astronomy, and medicine. He was a court alchemist during the reign of Caliph Haroun Al-Rashid and the physician to the grand ministers (viziers), the Barmakids. He authored many books that were translated into Latin during the Middle Ages (Amr & Tbakhi, 2007).

Figure 1.2: An Interpretive Depiction of Alchemical Traditions in Early Science

The book *Kitab al-Zuhra* (*Book of Venus*) on the noble art of alchemy was one of Jabir's prominent works. He also authored chemistry books such as *Kitab al-Kimya* (*Book of Chemistry*) and *Kitab Al-Sabe'en* (*The Seventy Books*) (Amr & Tbakhi, 2007). Jabir is believed to have introduced experimental methodology to alchemy and invented several processes still used in modern chemistry. Some of those processes are crystallization, calcination, sublimation, synthesis of acids like tartaric acid, and evaporation. He could also prepare various substances, such as steel, varnish for waterproof cloth, rust-prevention, and manganese dioxide for glassmaking (Amr & Tbakhi, 2007). He made aqua regia, which is used to dissolve gold. Aqua regia is a mixture of nitric acid and hydrochloric acid in a 1:3 ratio. All these practices are relevant to modern chemistry.

Scientific Revolution

The Scientific Revolution occurred, shifting chemistry from a mystical practice, such as alchemy, to an empirical science. The significant changes resulted from the Scientific Revolution during the 16th and 17th centuries (Brush, Spencer, & Osler, 2025). The long-standing Greek view of science was replaced by a more observation-based view of nature. Additionally, science gained autonomy from both philosophy and technology and began to be viewed as a separate discipline. The Aristotelian (Greek) worldview of science was the dominant view before the Scientific Revolution (Ignatik, n.d.). It focused on theoretical understanding rather than the practical application of scientific knowledge, and the practitioners called themselves 'natural philosophers'. They observed their surroundings and as much of the universe as they could to find meaning and purpose. However, the Scientific Revolution brought about a desire for precise observation, as seen in the work of Copernicus in the 16th century, instead of relying entirely on Aristotelian scientific concepts. The shift continued in the 17th century with scientists such as Galileo, who began to emphasize the practical application of scientific knowledge (Ignatik, n.d.). In summary, there was a break from Aristotelian tradition and the emergence of science as a structured, practical discipline grounded in the scientific method.

There are figures who were influential in shifting chemistry from mystical or magic-based roots to modern chemistry known today. One such figure is Robert Boyle, who published the book *The Sceptical Chymist* in 1661. The book is widely credited with separating chemistry from alchemy. Boyle challenged the traditional alchemical theories by emphasizing empirical evidence and experimental methods, laying the foundation for a scientific approach to chemical study. However, this highlights alchemy as the ancestral root of chemistry.

How Did Chemistry Become Organized and a Recognized Discipline?

The formation of chemical societies (groups) significantly encourages the development of chemistry education through collaboration and establishing professional standards (Knight, 1992). Key figures such as Humphry Davy and Justus von Liebig contributed through their involvement in these societies, promoting laboratory instruction and public lectures. Their efforts helped transform chemistry from a craft-based practice into a recognized scientific discipline.

Rise of Chemistry as an Academic Subject

In 1761, chemistry was not considered a true science, unlike physics, which was advanced by the work of the famous scientist Isaac Newton a century earlier. Chemistry was rooted in the alchemical tradition and the legacy of Greek philosophers (American Chemical Society International Historic Chemical Landmarks, n.d.). For instance, the four elements of Aristotle: earth, air, fire, and water, were considered the components that make up substances. However, some modifications to those elements were made by medieval alchemists, who added their own arcane language and symbolism. The shift from alchemy to modern chemistry can be seen through Antoine Laurent Lavoisier. This is evident in his work on combustion, which was originally viewed through the concept of phlogiston developed by the German scientist Georg Ernst Stahl in the early eighteenth century.

This concept states that combustible substances contain a component, or element, called phlogiston, and that when substances burn, they lose that component (American Chemical Society International Historic Chemical Landmarks, n.d.). Lavoisier tested the concept of phlogiston by burning phosphorus and sulfur and observed that weight was gained rather than lost, or that phlogiston was neither released nor lost. This contradicted the idea of phlogiston being lost during combustion. Lavoisier discovered that air was actually involved in combustion. This caused the scientist to conclude that phlogiston was imaginary and unscientific. This laid the foundation of the modern combustion concept based on oxygen and also modern chemistry. Lavoisier emphasized chemistry should be grounded in facts and direct observation.

Chemistry continued to develop until it became a university discipline. This is obvious because education in the 17th and 18th centuries differed from what it is today. Interestingly, many European universities of that period were established in the 13th century with a theoretical or humanistic foundation (Larson, 2020). Therefore, the focus was on teaching and studying areas of knowledge such as philosophy, medicine, logic, theology, law, mathematics, astronomy, and grammar. The educational model in those universities was viewed as stagnant, while scientific discoveries required adaptability, which was not typical of the humanities. However, chemistry became associated with and taught alongside medicine and pharmacy, making medical students the first to receive an education in chemistry in early America. Eventually, the first undergraduate chemistry course was taught in 1757 in the United States, and the first chemistry chair was appointed in 1769 at the College of Philadelphia (Larson, 2020). The Germans had more success with their educational model in promoting chemistry.

Many European and American chemists studied in Germany throughout the 19th century due to its academic freedom, seminars, and laboratories (Larson, 2020). The United States adopted the German model and research universities, but chemistry was not taught to high school students or even at the secondary education level during the 19th century. When chemistry was taught, it was primarily to white male students. Even after becoming well established, chemistry was considered a genteel discipline or a discipline for the elite, and not significantly practical until the Industrial Revolution. The Industrial Revolution increased the number of chemistry students and changed the image of the discipline. This is seen in the strong demand by industries for chemistry students at the start of the 20th century. Finally, mass education in America led subjects such as chemistry, biology, and physics to develop into their own schools of thought during the 19th and 20th centuries (Larson, 2020). This signaled the establishment of chemistry as an academic discipline.

Nineteenth-Century Reforms that Impact Chemistry Education

As mentioned earlier, the Industrial Revolution encouraged the growth of chemistry and helped make it a mainstream academic discipline. Industrialization during the nineteenth century increased the need for more people with knowledge of chemistry. The Industrial Revolution is a historical period that began in eighteenth-century Great Britain, leading to significant changes such as new innovations, tools, and machines (Wilkinson, 2024). There were advancements in metallurgy, for instance, furnaces that separated coal and prevented contamination of metals in a process called puddling. The Industrial Revolution is commonly stated as the period between 1750 and 1850, and cotton production was important to Britain's economic development. Cotton production progressed from small-scale cottage industry to large factory-based production.

Figure 1.3: Depicting the Industrial Revolution — The Hope and Despair

This progress in cotton production resulted from devices such as the spinning jenny, spinning mule, and power loom (Wilkinson, 2024). The power loom transitioned from human power to steam power. Additionally, the demand for bleaching solutions for cotton and other manufactured textiles gave rise to other research separate from the quest for artificial dyes. For example, research focused on explosives, solvents, fertilizers, and medicine. Eventually, in the second half of the nineteenth century, Germany emerged as a leader in industrial chemistry (Wilkinson, 2024). All these developments required an increasing number of people with knowledge of chemistry.

The expansion of secondary education in the nineteenth and early twentieth centuries led to the inclusion of chemistry in high school curricula across Europe and North America. This development established chemistry as a core academic discipline and promoted laboratory-based instruction to foster scientific understanding. During this same period, pioneering institutions began admitting women to chemistry programs, expanding access to scientific education. Ida Freund, appointed in 1890, became the first woman to hold a permanent university position in the United Kingdom, teaching chemistry (Moseley, 2001). She worked at Newnham College, Cambridge, until her retirement in 1912, and her teaching innovations and textbooks significantly influenced chemistry education. These milestones helped diversify the field and strengthened the foundation of modern chemistry education.

Challenges in Chemistry Education

Chemistry education, particularly at the secondary and tertiary levels, faces persistent challenges that affect student engagement, skill development, and long-term career outcomes. One major issue is the misalignment between educational content and the practical demands of the job market. Graduate programs tend to emphasize academic career paths, even though tenure-track positions are increasingly scarce. This narrow focus leaves students underprepared for roles in industry, government, and interdisciplinary research settings (National Research Council, 2012). Compounding this issue is the limited exposure students have to alternative career paths and the lack of soft skills training in areas such as communication, teamwork, and leadership. These challenges begin early in the education system, where chemistry is often taught abstractly with little connection to real-world applications, contributing to student disengagement and high attrition rates.

The landscape of chemistry education has also changed due to declining demand for chemists in traditional roles and a shift in interest toward more applied fields. In the 1970s, nearly twenty million individuals were employed as chemistry graduates during the height of U.S. manufacturing (National Research Council, 2012). This number declined significantly by the 2000s and was further impacted by the 2008 economic recession. Although the number of chemistry graduates has since improved, job prospects have not fully recovered. Chemist unemployment remains lower than the national average, but overall employment opportunities are more limited than in the past.

Many graduates now face difficult choices such as pursuing academic careers with modest salaries ranging from U.S. $75,000 to U.S. $92,000, or transitioning to higher-paying professional fields like dentistry or pharmacy, which offer starting salaries between U.S. $150,000 and U.S. $300,000 but often come with greater student debt (National Research Council, 2012). Automation, outsourcing, and changing industrial needs are factors that further influence the decline in traditional chemistry roles, reducing opportunities for graduate chemists who are increasingly being replaced by technology. However, job prospects for PhD chemistry graduates will be more promising in small or start-up companies, which are becoming increasingly attractive career options for these degree holders.

Caribbean Secondary Education Certificate (CSEC) Chemistry
The Caribbean Examinations Council (CXC) was established in 1972 through the collaborative agreement of fifteen English-speaking Caribbean countries to form a regional examination body suited to the region's developmental needs (CXC, n.d.-b). The twelve full member states include Antigua and Barbuda, Barbados, Belize, Dominica, Grenada, Guyana, Jamaica, Montserrat, St. Kitts and Nevis, St. Lucia, St. Vincent and the Grenadines, and Trinidad and Tobago. The associate members are Anguilla, the British Virgin Islands, and the Cayman Islands. CXC was created to replace external examinations with assessments that reflect the Caribbean's cultural, economic, and educational realities, such as British General Certificate of Education (GCE) examinations. The Council's mission is to develop human capital in the Caribbean by delivering high-quality syllabuses and valid, reliable, and internationally recognized examinations and certifications (CXC, n.d.-a). Its vision is to become a digitally transformed, globally competitive organization that provides relevant educational services to the region (CXC, n.d.-a).

One of the principal examinations offered by CXC is the Caribbean Secondary Education Certificate (CSEC), which serves as the terminal assessment for students completing secondary school. The purpose of the CSEC examination is to evaluate students' academic proficiency, analytical reasoning, and practical skills. Assessment is conducted through a combination of externally administered written papers and internally completed School-Based Assessments (SBAs), which are moderated by CXC to ensure regional standardization and fairness (CXC, n.d.-c). The examination covers a broad range of subjects, including English, Mathematics, Chemistry, Information Technology, Geography, and Technical Drawing. Through this framework, CXC plays a vital role in guiding students toward tertiary education, employment, or technical training, reinforcing its mandate as the leading certifying body for secondary-level education in the Caribbean.

The project is centered around an educator's experience with teaching CSEC chemistry, including the syllabus and the practical component (SBA). The subject of chemistry is taught to help students understand the physical and chemical properties of substances, and how matter and energy interact (CXC, n.d.-d). The subject aims to provide students with a sound understanding of everyday life, nature, technology, the importance of human well-being, and the environment from the perspective of chemistry. CSEC chemistry is designed to allow students to work individually and collaboratively in practical activities. Additionally, fieldwork and interactive activities such as group work and discussions should be connected to theoretical concepts to promote deeper understanding. This approach is intended to facilitate the use of investigative and problem-solving skills and to help students communicate scientific information effectively.

The syllabus encourages the use of various teaching and learning strategies and aims to cater to different student learning styles. CSEC chemistry is divided into three sections: Section A – Principles of Chemistry, Section B – Organic Chemistry, and Section C – Inorganic Chemistry. Twenty percent (20%) of the total marks for the CSEC chemistry examination is allocated to the school-based assessment (SBA), which students complete internally at their schools (CXC, n.d.-d). The remaining eighty percent (80%) is awarded based on the external written examination, consisting of Paper 1 (multiple choice) and Paper 2 (structured response).

It is important to note the low pass rates in CXC examinations, which are a growing concern. Many students continue to struggle with subjects like mathematics, English, and the sciences. These results point to deeper issues in how the curriculum is delivered and understood. There are also concerns about students' readiness and the level of support they receive. The situation suggests that urgent attention is needed to improve teaching methods and learning outcomes. This book hopes to address this problem specifically for chemistry. How will this book seek to accomplish that? This book will examine how reflective practices, class evaluations, and analyses of student work and teaching materials can inform improvements in the overall delivery and effectiveness of CSEC Chemistry instruction.

Statement of Problem

The instruction of CSEC Chemistry remains a significant challenge in many secondary classrooms. Students often struggle to understand fundamental concepts, resulting in low performance and limited retention. At the same time, many teachers find it difficult to complete the syllabus on time, which hinders effective content delivery. In some cases, teachers themselves struggle to master the very concepts they are required to teach and are unable to present the content in a way students can understand. This contributes to a lack of clarity, reduced engagement, and missed opportunities for meaningful learning.

Furthermore, many students fail to develop a genuine interest in chemistry, perceiving it as abstract and irrelevant. These challenges underscore the need for pedagogical approaches that are both effective and contextually relevant. Reflective practice by teachers can serve as a powerful tool to improve instructional strategies, making chemistry more comprehensible and engaging for students.

Purpose of the Book

The purpose of this book is to analyze existing instructional materials and student work from a secondary chemistry classroom to identify pedagogical strengths and weaknesses. It also seeks to align teaching strategies with established learning theories and styles and to develop new instructional resources based on these insights. The book will further explore classroom management practices and evaluate how adjustments can improve engagement. The overall goal is to demonstrate how teacher-driven reflection and research can lead to meaningful and sustainable improvements in science teaching.

Research Questions

- What teaching strengths and weaknesses are revealed through analysis of past lesson plans, homework, and classroom activities?
- Which learning theories and learning styles are represented in these classroom materials?
- How can classroom evaluations and management strategies inform improved teaching practice?

Significance of the Book

This research is significant because it uses real classroom data and focuses on continuous, practice-based improvement. It offers a grounded model for professional growth by integrating theory with lived classroom experience. The findings will contribute to the field of chemistry education by providing a roadmap for teachers seeking to enhance instruction through reflective methods and the application of educational theory. It will also demonstrate how teachers can use their own classrooms as sites of research and transformation.

Context of the Book

CSEC Chemistry instruction poses ongoing challenges, including difficulties in concept comprehension, syllabus completion, and student engagement. Teachers often work under time constraints and struggle to cover the entire content effectively. At the same time, students find it difficult to connect with the subject and develop meaningful and lasting interest. This book is grounded in real-world data from secondary school teachers and students. It explores how reflective practice and the analysis of classroom materials, such as lesson plans, assignments, and teacher notes, can support meaningful, contextually relevant improvements in science education.

Chapter 1

Literature Review

Chemistry, or chemical education, is the study of the teaching and learning of chemistry to better address its abstract nature, which makes it difficult to learn (University of Oxford, Department of Chemistry, n.d.). Therefore, it focuses on creating and studying models of learning and teaching chemistry at all levels, from elementary to university. Several key components of chemistry education were identified by analyzing the available information and selecting the most critical aspects for emphasis. These components are presented in Table 1.

Component	**Academic Description**
Conceptual Learning and Modeling	Students form and refine explanations for chemical phenomena such as relating observations to atomic-level interactions.
Misconceptions and Threshold Concepts	Educators identify and correct incorrect beliefs and emphasize ideas that are essential but challenging to learn.
Laboratory Skills Development	Students practice hands-on tasks such as titration, filtration, and heating, while following safety protocols.
Cognitive Load in Practical Work	Teachers reduce excessive mental demands in practical sessions through planning, clear instructions, and guidance.
Assessment and Feedback	Both informal and formal evaluations are used to give feedback, guide learning, and adjust teaching strategies.
Curriculum Structure and Progression	Content is arranged to build progressively from basic to complex ideas, supporting deeper understanding.
Technology Integration	Digital simulations, animations, and virtual labs enhance visualization and allow safe exploration of reactions.

Component	Academic Description
Societal and Real-World Contexts	Chemistry is taught through current global issues like pollution, pharmaceuticals, and sustainability.
Student Motivation and Engagement	Teachers use real-life examples and active strategies to increase student interest and persistence in learning.
Inclusivity and Differentiation	Instruction is adapted to support students with varying abilities, backgrounds, and needs.
Communication and Scientific Literacy	Students are taught to write lab reports, explain results, and present findings using scientific terms and logic.

Table 2.1: The Components of Chemistry Education

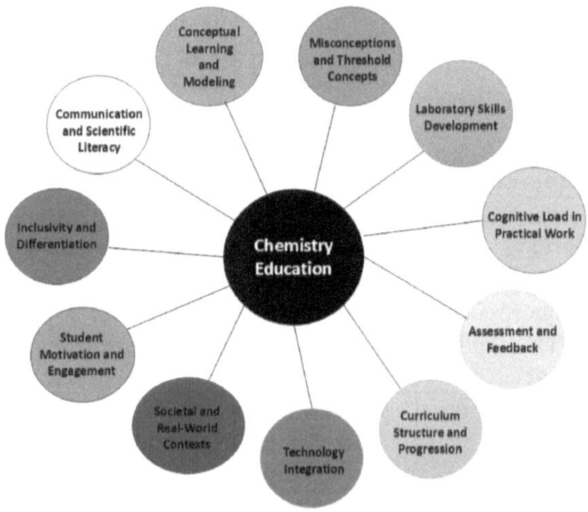

Figure 2.1: The Core Component of Chemistry Education

Component of Chemistry Education

Conceptual Learning and Modeling

Conceptual learning and modeling refer to building and improving the mental models used to explain chemical processes (concepts) at the macroscopic, submicroscopic, and symbolic levels (Taber, 2013). Taber (2013) called the macroscopic, submicroscopic, and symbolic relationship "the chemistry triplet" or "Johnstone's model." The chemistry triplet describes chemical understanding across three levels: macroscopic (what we see, such as colour changes), submicroscopic (what happens at the particle level, such as atoms bonding), and symbolic (how we represent it, such as equations and formulas). For example, a student can learn about the dissolution of salt by making observations. At the macroscopic level, the student observes that the salt disappears and the solution remains colorless. At the submicroscopic level, the student explains that dissolution occurs due to ion-dipole interactions between sodium and chloride ions and water molecules. Finally, at the symbolic level, diagrams or chemical equations can be used to represent the dissociation process and the interaction between ions and water.

Misconceptions and Threshold Concepts

There are numerous misconceptions that plague chemistry, especially during the earlier periods of students' education. For example, chemical or chemistry education research shows that students hold misconceptions, such as atoms in molecules are touching or mass disappears during combustion (Barke et al., 2009). Additionally, if students master certain concepts referred to as 'threshold concepts,' such as atomic theory, chemical bonding, intermolecular forces, and chemical equilibrium, their understanding of chemistry improves in unimaginable ways (Talanquer, 2015). The students become better able to understand and communicate chemistry by overcoming the abstract barrier that hinders understanding of the subject.

Laboratory Skills Development

Chemistry students must develop good laboratory skills to survive in the discipline. The laboratory skills demonstrated are closely associated with the application of theoretical knowledge in simulated real-world settings, such as schools, or in actual real-world settings, such as a company during an internship. The students apply techniques they will use if they continue in the discipline or closely related fields. Some of the techniques taught at the secondary level and higher, such as titration, distillation, and chromatography require students to possess manual dexterity, procedural understanding, and keen attention to safety. The adherence to effective laboratory instruction promotes technical proficiency and metacognitive reflection (a form of self-reflection) on the experimental design and outcomes (Hofstein & Lunetta, 2004). A demonstration of good laboratory skill is the proper performance of a titration experiment, which requires the understanding of endpoint indicators, molar calculations, and proper use of burettes. Those skills transform the students into individuals capable of scientific precision, observation, and patience.

Cognitive Load in Practical Work

The laboratory environment can place cognitive load on students, especially when they are required to simultaneously recall theory, follow complex steps, and operate unfamiliar equipment (Johnstone & Al-Shuaili, 2001). Therefore, individuals who are just learning chemistry may have difficulty associating theory with observation and discerning observations due to interference from instruments, which hinders their learning. The teacher can lessen cognitive load by conducting visual demonstrations, segmenting procedures where possible, and supporting students during the execution of the experiment. For example, the teacher can provide a video recording of the experiment for students to watch and study to be better equipped to perform the experiment. This facilitates memorization and promotes meaningful learning.

Assessment and Feedback

The effective assessment of students is an essential aspect of chemical education, which facilitates the monitoring of progress, guides teaching, and enables student reflection (Black & Wiliam, 2009). Formative assessments include quizzes, concept maps, and oral questioning. The teacher uses formative assessment to adapt their teaching based on feedback and data obtained, such as identifying gaps in knowledge or misconceptions. On the other hand, student mastery or cumulative understanding is evaluated using summative assessments such as lab reports or standardized tests. Feedback from formative assessment must be specific, timely, and actionable. For example, pointing out a student's error in applying the ideal gas law, along with a corrective explanation, helps reinforce the correct approach and reduces future errors.

Curriculum Structure and Progression

Effective chemistry curricula are sequenced to build from basic to advanced concepts, helping students develop coherent, connected understandings. Vertical alignment of the curriculum can ensure this by structuring content to be cohesive, consistent, and in accordance with stipulated standards (Center for Comprehensive School Reform and Improvement, 2009). It also reduces repetition, especially across grade levels, and ensures that teachers progress from basic to advanced concepts, such as from atomic structure to chemical bonding. Additionally, horizontal integration can be used to further enhance learning by teaching related subjects or concepts simultaneously, allowing students to make connections across disciplines (Wijnen-Meijer, 2019). For example, teaching catalysts in chemistry and enzymes in biology at the same time supports the understanding that enzymes are biological catalysts.

A poorly structured curriculum risks cognitive dissonance, as students may encounter abstract ideas without sufficient foundational knowledge. Curriculum frameworks like the Next Generation Science Standards (NGSS) exemplify progression from concrete to abstract learning outcomes in chemistry education. This means students first engage in hands-on experiences, such as dissolving sugar in water, before being taught conceptual knowledge, including the dissolution of solids in water and the use of symbolic representations.

Technology Integration

Technology enhances chemical education by making abstract concepts visible and interactive. Tools such as molecular simulations, spectroscopy apps, and virtual labs allow students to explore phenomena that are difficult to observe directly (Suits & Sanger, 2013). For example, a simulation of molecular vibrations helps students visualize IR spectroscopy peaks. Online reaction modeling platforms also offer safe environments to explore synthesis without the constraints of physical resources. Integrating such tools improves conceptual understanding and student engagement, especially in resource-limited or remote learning environments.

Figure 2.2: A Depiction of Technology Integration

Societal and Real-World Contexts

Chemistry can be made relevant to students by connecting the discipline to real-world and societal issues. Additionally, it promotes critical thinking and sparks curiosity and interest in the subject. For example, teaching topics such as air pollution, green chemistry, drug development, and climate change can help students understand how chemistry impacts their lives and addresses current global challenges, ultimately motivating them to learn the discipline (King, 2012). For instance, the concept of acid rain can be taught from the perspective of industrial emissions released into the environment, which alter the pH of rainwater and render it acidic. This acidic rainwater then undergoes chemical reactions with materials such as metals and marble, leading to structural damage. The environmental consequences of acid rain, including its effects on soil health, are also mentioned and discussed. Socio-scientific issues such as damage to soil health and climate change allow students to consider ethical and cultural perspectives, thereby fostering responsible citizenship. These contexts transform chemistry from abstract content into a meaningful tool for understanding the world.

Student Motivation and Engagement

Motivation is a key factor in sustaining student effort and achievement in chemistry. Engaging students through hands-on activities, gamified assessments, and real-life applications boosts interest and participation (Ryan & Deci, 2000). For instance, students learning about osmosis by placing slices of an Irish potato in saltwater can observe the effects firsthand, making abstract concepts more tangible. Similarly, allowing students to witness diffusion by placing potassium permanganate crystals in a beaker of water the day before the lesson sets the stage for inquiry and deep engagement. Teachers who create supportive learning environments and encourage autonomy help develop intrinsic motivation. Engaged learners are more likely to persevere through difficult topics and develop a lasting interest in science.

According to Ryan and Deci (2000), intrinsic motivation refers to doing an activity for its inherent satisfaction, such as curiosity or enjoyment. Extrinsic motivation involves performing an activity to attain a separable outcome, such as rewards or approval. For instance, a student who conducts an experiment out of a genuine interest in chemical reactions demonstrates intrinsic motivation, whereas one who studies only to earn high grades or praise from parents is extrinsically motivated. Although both types can drive behavior, intrinsic motivation is often linked to deeper learning and long-term engagement. Educators can foster this by offering meaningful choices, acknowledging student perspectives, and connecting content to students' lives.

Inclusivity and Differentiation

Diversity in science education is multifaceted and cannot be easily defined, as it encompasses a wide range of student differences that influence academic engagement and achievement. These differences may include cultural background, socioeconomic status, language proficiency, immigrant experience, gender identity, and sexual orientation (Kousa & Aksela, 2019). Additionally, students may enter the classroom with varied cognitive abilities, learning disabilities, or psychological challenges, each of which affects how they engage with the curriculum. For example, a student from a non-English-speaking household might struggle with technical vocabulary in chemistry, while another with dyslexia may benefit from audio-based resources and simplified lab instructions. Teachers who implement differentiated strategies, such as offering visual diagrams alongside written content or allowing oral assessments, can more effectively support students with diverse learning needs.

In chemistry education specifically, these diversity-related challenges can contribute to high attrition rates, especially among students from underrepresented backgrounds (Villafañe, Jang, and Lewis, 2021). It was further indicated that students often leave chemistry programs due to a perceived lack of belonging and the subject's intimidating nature. Creating inclusive environments through culturally responsive teaching and accessible instruction can counteract these trends. For instance, including examples of scientific contributions from various cultures or allowing students to investigate chemical reactions using familiar local substances such as vinegar and baking soda for acid-base reactions can make learning more relatable. By actively acknowledging and valuing diversity, educators can reduce barriers to learning and promote greater equity and persistence in science education.

Communication and Scientific Literacy

Chemical education must foster students' ability to communicate scientifically. In the scientific community, persons who can communicate effectively orally and in writing are generally successful in gaining recognition and support from their peers (Yore, Hand, & Florence, 2004, abstract). Some forms in which scientists disseminate their findings or research include research articles, grant proposals, poster presentations, and scientific tasks (Hutchins, 2020). Also, the audience, purpose, format, and the significance of the research must be considered when preparing scientific communication to ensure appropriateness. Students should learn to describe results with precision, justify claims with evidence, and follow conventions of scientific language. For example, in a lab report on reaction rates, students must state the hypothesis, describe the procedures clearly, present the data in tables, and discuss the results logically. Scientific literacy prepares students for further study, research, and informed participation in public science debates.

According to Hutchins (2020), effective scientific communication begins with a careful analysis of three elements: audience, purpose, and format. For students, this involves understanding that a formal lab report differs in tone and detail from a public-facing science poster or newsletter article. Scientific writing must also be tailored to the knowledge level of the intended audience. When communicating with nonexperts, students should avoid technical jargon, use simple language, and include visuals to convey meaning clearly. For instance, a student explaining chemical equilibrium in a poster might rely on analogies and charts to simplify the concept. Finally, Hutchins (2020) stresses the importance of research storytelling. Rather than simply listing procedures and results, students should learn to present their work as a logical narrative, highlighting the significance of the study and its broader implications. This approach not only improves communication skills but also deepens students' understanding of the scientific process.

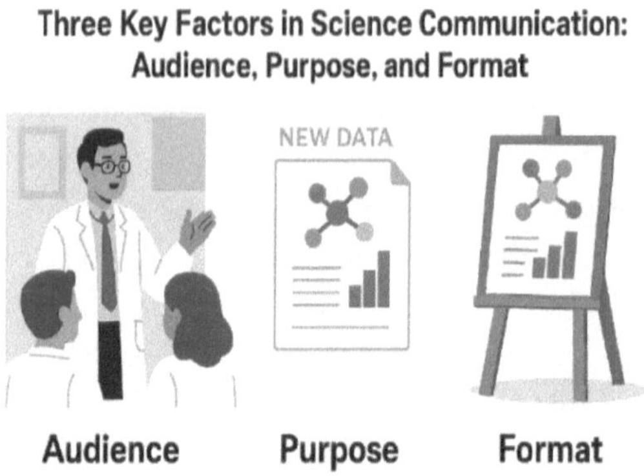

Figure 2.3: Key Factors in Science Communication

The Present Status of Chemistry Education across the Globe

The field of chemistry education is transitioning from personal empiricism to one grounded in learning theories supported by evidence to improve teaching and learning (Sweeder, Herrington, & Crandell, 2023). What does personal empiricism really mean? Personal empiricism refers to a reliance on individual experiences, intuition, or informal observations rather than systematic research or established learning theories to guide teaching practices. This shift reflects a growing recognition that chemistry teaching must not only convey factual knowledge but also foster critical thinking, problem-solving, and real-world application skills to prepare students for career opportunities. Unfortunately, chemistry education as an academic discipline is declining internationally, as seen in universities in Japan, Australia, Europe, and the United States (Price & Hill, 2004). Additionally, the prestige once associated with chemistry has significantly declined, and some reasons have been given to counter this decline. For instance, chemistry is useful in everyday life; everyone should have knowledge of science, and science is worth studying because it is science.

The field of research dedicated to studying chemistry education is called chemistry education research (CER). CER scholars caution that without robust institutional support, evidence-based methods risk limited classroom adoption or use in the classroom, especially in regions lacking funding or training infrastructure. The decline in chemistry is attributed to its ubiquity or unclear identity (Price & Hill, 2004). This makes chemistry seem irrelevant to the average person, who cannot clearly see its practicality. Therefore, parents are less likely to encourage their children to pursue chemistry research in Japan, as shown.

Additionally, chemistry is more likely to be blamed for problems such as pollution, while other disciplines are credited for accomplishments in chemistry, such as the development of new cancer drugs. Chemistry involves a significant amount of mathematics, which is a major deterrent to studying the discipline. Educational studies show that math anxiety is particularly pronounced in chemistry contexts, reducing student motivation and achievement. However, "dumbing down" chemistry, as seen in the university Chemistry I course (introductory chemistry), should not be the solution. Also, more and more students are choosing other careers, and chemistry is being diluted as a service subject because key concepts are omitted to fit the needs of non-chemistry students.

Profound challenges are also evident in secondary education globally. For example, teachers often lack subject specialization and resources which hinder effective chemistry instruction. For example, over half of physics and chemistry classes in some Brazilian regions are taught by non-specialist teachers (Teixeira, da Silva, & de Souza, 2012). A study from North Macedonia revealed that insufficient lab equipment, outdated curricula, and limited teacher training severely impede student learning in secondary schools (Stojanovska, Mijić, & Petruševski, 2020). While chemistry education is evolving through evidence-based practices, global disparities remain pronounced. In many African and South Asian regions, limited infrastructure, overcrowded classrooms, and insufficient teacher training hinder effective science instruction (UNESCO, 2023). This trend is compounded by the global shortage of qualified chemistry teachers, particularly in rural and underserved communities. Expanding international collaboration and funding is crucial to reversing these declines and supporting equitable access to quality chemistry education.

The global status of chemistry can be increased again by raising public awareness of the discipline's contributions to society and by addressing negative imagery, such as its association with pollution (Price & Hill, 2004). The integration of research into the curriculum can help attract more students and make the curriculum more hands-on. Additionally, students and lecturers can work side by side through an apprenticeship to enable mutual dialogue. The physical nature of chemistry should be emphasized to counter the significant amount of mathematics. Also, when chemistry is not taught in a cohesive and comprehensive manner, key concepts are often absorbed by other disciplines such as pharmacology and materials science, which then gain prominence while chemistry itself risks diminishing in stature.

On the other hand, modern innovations such as virtual labs, augmented reality simulations, and inquiry-based digital platforms are reshaping chemistry education in high-income regions (National Research Council, 2021). However, the integration of these tools is uneven due to resource and training gaps. Sustained professional development for teachers, especially in low-resource settings, is essential to enable the adoption of such technologies and pedagogies (OECD, 2022). Additionally, interdisciplinary curricula that connect chemistry to sustainability, health, and social issues are increasingly important for student engagement. Addressing curriculum rigidity and enhancing teacher agency will support a more dynamic, inclusive, and relevant chemistry education system worldwide.

It must be known that chemistry produces professionals capable of taking what nature produces and converting those substances into products beneficial to humans, directly or indirectly (Nature, 2022)—for example, drugs, dyes, fertilizers, and food packaging. Ironically, the main environmental issues are closely linked to chemistry, such as carbon emissions and plastic pollution. However, the discipline of chemistry is seeking to solve those problems using innovative solutions. Researchers in chemistry education advocate for curricula grounded in a systems-thinking approach, enabling students to understand the interconnections within chemical compounds or products and to evaluate chemistry's broader impacts on the economy, society, environment, and human health. Such systems thinking curricula have been shown to improve student engagement, interdisciplinary collaboration, and sustainability literacy.

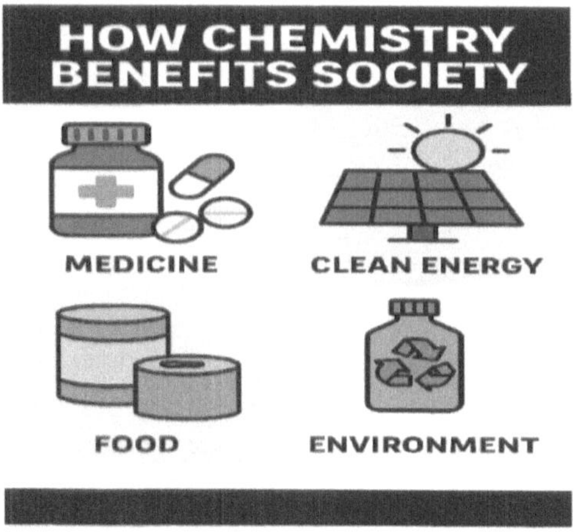

Figure 2.4: Chemistry and Society: Everyday Benefits

Universities and professional chemistry organizations are taking steps to drive change in the discipline (Nature, 2022). For instance, Imperial College London has suspended its long-standing master's programs in petroleum engineering and petroleum geoscience. The American Chemical Society actively promotes sustainable chemistry education through research and outreach, emphasizing systems thinking. Similarly, the Royal Society of Chemistry (RSC) has acknowledged that current school curricula fall short in preparing students for challenges related to climate change and sustainability, and it has called for significant educational reforms. Nonetheless, obstacles remain to implementing such reforms, such as curriculum rigidity, resource limitations, and inadequate assessment tools, especially at the secondary level. Also, university-level initiatives often lack coordination with schools.

Chemistry encompasses several specialized branches, each with its own focus and real-world applications. Introducing these areas at the secondary level helps students see the relevance of chemistry to everyday life, future careers, and global challenges. Some of those specialized branches are:

1. Analytical chemistry: This field focuses on measuring and identifying substances. It is used in medical labs to test blood, diagnose diseases, and detect contaminants.
2. Biochemistry: This area studies the chemistry of living things. It helps develop vaccines and understand how the body works.
3. Chemical engineering: This field applies chemistry, math, and engineering. It is used to design processes that make fuels, clean water, and plastics.
4. Inorganic chemistry: This branch studies metals and non-carbon compounds. It is important for making batteries, fertilizers, and metal-based drugs.
5. Organic chemistry: This field focuses on carbon-based compounds. It is used to make medicines, cosmetics, and food additives.
6. Physical chemistry: This area examines how chemical reactions occur. It helps improve solar panels and battery technology.

The State of Chemistry Education in the Caribbean: Trends and Implications

In the Caribbean region, university enrollment in science programs has experienced a decline. There are numerous factors on the ground influencing this decline, as revealed by analysis. For example, in Jamaica, sixty-eight percent (68%) of scientific papers have foreign co-authors. This is blamed on the lack of research facilities and equipment needed to conduct basic research and research with far-reaching impact (Singh Wilmot, 2024). Practices such as inviting overseas collaborators to join projects without making intellectual contributions have arisen just to gain access to equipment. Also, Jamaican scientists often depend on funding from international sources, which can influence research directions not aligned with Jamaica's goals.

Additionally, postgraduate students face the same issue: limited access to funding and essential resources, such as equipment. The outcome of the lack of funding and other resources leads to a decline in enrollment at universities, long completion times, and even abandonment of research projects (Singh Wilmot, 2024). Also, STEM students migrate for opportunities such as graduate work overseas and the opportunity to participate in innovation. This highlights issues affecting STEM education, specifically chemistry, at the tertiary level in the Caribbean, using Jamaica as an example.

The decline in enrollment in chemistry programmes at universities in the Caribbean can be linked to what is happening at the secondary level of education in the Caribbean. There is a frightening trend of limited awareness of career prospects, low secondary school performance in science, and the increasing preference for business studies and technology disciplines. It is secondary education students who are expected to transition to the university level to pursue studies, yet a decline in student enrollment is being seen at universities. For example, institutions like the University of the West Indies (UWI) have reported a decline in enrollment; for example, student enrollment declined from 19,052 in 2020–2021 to 16,338 students in 2022–2023 (University of the

West Indies, Mona, 2023). Science enrollment declined from 3,179 students in 2020–2021 to 2,875 students in 2022–2023. This shows a decline in STEM education, such as chemistry, in the Caribbean region. Additionally, the Caribbean is a region significantly affected by brain drain, the migration of many qualified students in search of better opportunities. For example, many trained teachers migrate for better opportunities, which affect education, including chemistry education, as seen in the teacher shortage in Jamaica (Jamaica Teachers' Association, 2025).

There are numerous negative factors affecting secondary school chemistry education, including teacher shortages, a shortage of specialist teachers, and limited resources, such as inadequate funding and laboratory facilities. The World Bank highlights the negative effects of these factors, as evidenced by only 4.9% of the 200,000 students passing five or more subjects upon sitting the CSEC examinations (Burunciuc, 2025). This has frustrated parents and teachers, which is a concern given the known link between education and negative social activities, such as crime. The World Bank highlighted issues in foundational learning, inequality in access to education, inadequate school resources, overcrowding in schools, underqualified or demotivated teachers, and even violence as factors negatively impacting access to quality education, leading to undesirable outcomes, as seen in the CSEC examination pass rate. It is important to clarify what is meant by 'foundational learning' before discussing ongoing measures to address the problem. Foundational learning involves basic literacy, numeracy, and transferable skills that are critical for further learning, especially as students' progress from the primary to secondary levels (Burunciuc, 2025). The lack of foundational learning restricts students' ability to engage in complex critical thinking, problem-solving, and creativity.

In essence, foundational learning can be associated with 21st-century skills in education. These skills refer to a broad set of competencies necessary for success in today's world, including critical thinking, problem-solving, communication, collaboration, digital literacy, and adaptability. The World Bank is assisting Caribbean nations to overcome the challenges affecting the quality of secondary education and to develop 21st-century skills. For example, the Education Public Expenditure Review (PER) studies conducted in Jamaica and Belize analyzed the efficiency and equity of education spending to compare them with regional and global standards (Burunciuc, 2025). The PER study gave Jamaica the analytical groundwork to establish its education project. The project is helping Jamaica improve teaching methods, upgrade secondary schools' facilities, and enhance educational management information systems to support better decision-making. Additionally, the World Bank has assisted Guyana in building more schools equipped with state-of-the-art technology to improve access to quality education and address overcrowding.

Within the scope of the Caribbean curriculum for secondary chemistry education, specifically CSEC Chemistry, progress towards making chemistry practical, relevant, and interdisciplinary can be observed. For example, green chemistry features in the CSEC Chemistry syllabus, allowing students to learn how chemistry is used to address environmental issues and to make substances less harmful to the environment. Also, the COVID-19 pandemic highlighted how chemistry can be taught virtually, which can be a short-term solution for schools with infrastructure limitations. Additionally, governments are investing in STEM education; STEM stands for Science, Technology, Engineering, and Mathematics. There are even virtual initiatives that provide resources to primary, secondary, and tertiary STEM learners to make learning those disciplines easier. The benefits also extend to teachers.

A critical gap exists between secondary-level chemistry education and university readiness in the Caribbean. Many tertiary instructors report that students entering chemistry programs lack fundamental laboratory skills and conceptual understanding, suggesting a misalignment between CSEC/CAPE content and university expectations. Leong, Mercer, Danczak, Kyne, and Thompson (2021, abstract) found that while secondary educators generally perceive their students as prepared, tertiary educators frequently observe deficiencies in core competencies, particularly in laboratory practice and scientific reasoning. Strengthening this transition requires clearer curricular alignment, early exposure to university-level laboratory environments, and initiatives such as dual-enrollment or summer bridge programs. Collaboration between secondary schools and universities through mentorship, outreach, and policy coordination can further promote smoother transitions. Building these linkages is essential for sustaining tertiary-level enrollment and performance in chemistry disciplines.

Chemistry Education in Caribbean Secondary Schools

Chemistry education at the Caribbean level is instruction primarily in accordance with the Caribbean Examinations Council (CXC) curriculum. CXC provides the curriculum and assessment for two major exams for secondary students in the Caribbean. Those examinations are the Caribbean Secondary Education Certificate (CSEC) and the Caribbean Advanced Proficiency Examination (CAPE). Those exams are accepted worldwide for admission into universities, colleges, and vocational schools. Universities accept these exams because they serve as regionally standardized academic benchmarks. The CSEC is considered equivalent to the General Certificate of Education Ordinary Level (GCE O-Level), while the CAPE is equivalent to the General Certificate of Education Advanced Level (GCE A-Level) used in the British education system. These internationally recognized equivalencies make CSEC and CAPE results valuable for both regional and overseas university admission processes.

In the case of Chemistry, students are assessed through a combination of written examinations and School-Based Assessments (SBAs). For CSEC Chemistry, students typically complete Paper 01 (multiple-choice), Paper 02 (structured questions), and a School-Based assessment (SBA). The SBA enables students to demonstrate their practical laboratory skills and their ability to plan and conduct scientific investigations. Similarly, CAPE Chemistry consists of Unit I and Unit II, each including internal SBA coursework and external examination papers that assess higher-order cognitive and analytical skills required for tertiary science education.

According to the Jamaica Information Service, the 2024 CSEC Chemistry pass rate in Jamaica was 64.1%, a modest figure when compared to 74.5% in Biology and 69.6% in Physics (JIS, 2024a). Regionally, the overall pass rate for CSEC Chemistry declined from 67% in 2023 to 64% in 2024, reflecting a slight decline from previous years (Kaieteur News, 2024). On the other hand, students sitting CAPE Chemistry have consistently maintained high levels of achievement. In 2024, CAPE Chemistry pass rates exceeded 90%, indicating strong academic performance among students at the advanced secondary level (JIS, 2024b). This performance might be related to the fact that students who sit CAPE will need to study those subjects to pursue medicine, engineering, law, and to gain admission into other programs that require CAPE. Thus, students are generally more motivated when they pursue CAPE.

This disparity in performance between CSEC and CAPE Chemistry underscores the need for strengthening foundational preparation at the CSEC level. Improved access to laboratory facilities, enhanced teacher support, and more interesting formative assessment practices may contribute to raising students' proficiency in Chemistry. Also, finding ways to motivate students for CSEC in the same way they are motivated for CAPE is another important approach to improve the CSEC Chemistry pass rate.

The Application of Learning Theories in Chemistry Education

There are numerous learning theories in education. This section explores some of the most effective learning theories in chemistry education. The learning theories discussed are constructivist learning theory, cognitive load theory, experiential learning theory, and social constructivism.

Constructivist Learning Theory

The constructivist learning theory holds that teachers cannot simply transmit knowledge to students; instead, students must actively construct knowledge for themselves (Bada, 2015). Basically, students learn by integrating new knowledge gained through cognition (learning) with what they already know. Some of the major contributors to the development of the theory are Dewey (1929), Bruner (1961), Vygotsky (1962), and Piaget (1980) (Bada, 2015).

Brief contributions of each theorist:

- Dewey (1929) emphasized learning through experience and reflection.
- Bruner (1961) introduced the concept of discovery learning, encouraging students to learn by doing.
- Vygotsky (1962) highlighted the importance of social interaction and the Zone of Proximal Development.
- Piaget (1980) focused on cognitive development stages and how learners actively construct knowledge based on these stages.

Constructivism is a theory of observation and scientific study that explains how people learn (Bada, 2015). People construct their understanding of the world based on prior knowledge and experiences. Students use what they already know to learn through active participation in the learning process, such as asking questions, reflecting on existing knowledge, conducting experiments, and solving real-world problems. Simply put, learning is an active, not a passive, process. Two core concepts in constructivism are assimilation and accommodation (Bada, 2015). Assimilation is when learners incorporate new information into their existing knowledge without changing their mental structures. For example, a child who knows dogs have four legs may call a cat a dog at first. In contrast, accommodation occurs when learners modify their existing knowledge to include new experiences. Using the previous example, the child eventually learns that cats and dogs are different animals that have four legs and adjusts their understanding accordingly.

In a constructivist classroom, knowledge and authority are shared between the teacher and students (Bada, 2015). Also, the teacher acts as a facilitator, and the student group is diverse or heterogeneous (Bada, 2015). For example, a teacher may present a science problem about climate change and ask students to work in groups to explore possible solutions. Students would then research, discuss, and present their findings, while the teacher guides their inquiry through questioning rather than direct instruction. This method promotes collaboration, critical thinking, and active knowledge construction, which are central to constructivist teaching. Similarly, in a chemistry classroom, the teacher might introduce the topic of acids and bases by asking students to test the pH of household substances like vinegar, baking soda, and soap. Students would work in groups, make observations, and construct their understanding of acids and bases through experimentation and discussion, while the teacher supports the process by asking probing questions rather than delivering direct explanations.

Cognitive Load Theory

The cognitive load theory describes memory as having three key parts: sensory, working, and long-term (Office of Educational Improvement, Medical College of Wisconsin, 2022). Sensory memory acts as a filter, blocking out most of what is occurring around us and passing select information to our working memory for further processing. Working memory can process 5 to 9 pieces of information at any given time. The working memory then categorizes information for storage in long-term memory or for discarding. Long-term memory stores information in structures called schemas, which are based on how information is used. Basically, the more you use the information, the more developed the schema becomes, making recall easier. The purpose of cognitive load is to prevent learners from being overloaded with more than they can process in the educational setting. For example, breaking problems into smaller parts can make it easier for learners to work on them rather than overwhelming them with a large, complex problem (Office of Educational Improvement, Medical College of Wisconsin, 2022).

In a chemistry class, a teacher might reduce cognitive load by teaching chemical equations in steps: first, introducing reactants and products; then teaching the rules for balancing equations; and finally applying those rules in practice problems. This helps students avoid cognitive overload by building their understanding progressively.

Experiential Learning Theory

Experiential learning theory is a type of constructivist learning theory which involves "learning by doing" (Experiential Learning, 2021). The learner must be doing something when this learning theory is applied, making this a type of active learning (the learner actively participates). The learning occurs through a continuous cycle of inquiry, reflection, analysis, and synthesis (Experiential Learning, 2021).

- Inquiry involves asking questions or exploring a problem, such as a student designing a chemistry experiment to test the effect of temperature on reaction rate.
- Reflection is the process of thinking about what happened, for example, a student reviewing why their experiment yielded unexpected results.
- Analysis involves breaking down and examining data or outcomes, such as interpreting a graph showing pH changes over time in a titration.
- Synthesis refers to combining ideas to form a new understanding, such as using experimental results to develop a procedure for neutralizing acidic waste.

David A. Kolb describes experiential learning as the transformation of experiences into knowledge (Experiential Learning, 2021). This allows learners to bridge the gap between theory and practice, such as real-world problem-solving, thereby shifting learning beyond the classroom. Kolb's experiential learning cycle consists of four main modes of learning: concrete experience, reflective observation, abstract conceptualization, and active experimentation (Experiential Learning, 2021). Concrete experience refers to direct involvement, like performing a chemical reaction in the lab. Reflective observation involves reviewing the experience, such as noting unexpected color changes. Abstract conceptualization includes forming theories, such as linking reaction outcomes to collision theory. Active experimentation is the application of new understanding, such as modifying a procedure to achieve greater yield in future trials.

Some examples of experiential learning activities in the classroom are applied research projects, case studies, field experiences, simulations, labs, and work-integrated learning (Experiential Learning, 2021).

- Applied research project: Students investigate water quality in local rivers using chemical testing.
- Case study: Learners analyze a real chemical spill and propose cleanup strategies.
- Field experience: Students visit a water treatment plant to observe chemical processes in action.
- Simulation: A virtual lab allows students to safely explore acid-base titrations.
- Lab: Learners conduct hands-on experiments to determine the molarity of solutions.
- Work-integrated learning: A student interns at a pharmaceutical lab and applies classroom knowledge to real-world chemical analysis.

Figure 2.5: Application of Knowledge from Classroom Learning to Real-World Setting

The image (figure 8) depicts students engaged in a field experience, collecting water samples from a river while wearing appropriate personal protective equipment, including lab coats, safety goggles, and water boots. This scene illustrates applied research activity, where students practice real-world scientific methods such as sampling, observation, and data collection in an authentic environmental setting. It reinforces experiential learning in Chemistry by connecting theoretical knowledge to environmental monitoring and problem-solving.

Social Constructivism (Vygotsky)

Social constructivism is a social learning theory developed by the Russian psychologist Lev Vygotsky. The theory presents learners as active participants in their own learning, knowledge acquisition, or knowledge creation (Davis, Witcraft, Baird, & Smits, 2017). Basically, Vygotsky does not view learning as taking place solely in the learner but rather primarily in a social and cultural setting. This means learning occurs mainly through social interactions with peers, teachers, and parents. Teachers are expected to stimulate and guide student interaction by using the natural flow of classroom conversations to facilitate learning, rather than forcing the direction of discussion. Social constructivism theory works best with dyads (groups of two) and small groups. Therefore, the theory emphasizes that successful learning depends heavily on interpersonal interactions and discussion, and the ultimate goal is to ensure that students understand these discussions (Davis, Witcraft, Baird, & Smits, 2017).

An important concept in social constructivism is the Zone of Proximal Development (ZPD), which helps define the role of educators or instructors in individual learning (Davis, Witcraft, Baird, & Smits, 2017). The ZPD differentiates between what the learner or student can learn on their own without help and what they cannot learn without the assistance and guidance of the teacher (educator or instructor). Basically, there are things students can master without help and others they cannot without support (Davis, Witcraft, Baird, & Smits, 2017). For example, in a chemistry class, a student may understand the basic concept of chemical reactions but needs teacher guidance to correctly balance chemical equations. With scaffolding, such as providing a partially completed equation, step-by-step examples, or guiding questions, the teacher supports the student until they can apply the balancing rules independently. These supports are gradually reduced as the student's competence increases.

Examples of social constructivism in the classroom include students working in pairs to design an experiment, predict its outcome based on prior knowledge, and then discuss their findings together. Another example is a group discussion where learners evaluate the environmental impact of different chemical products, with the teacher facilitating rather than directing the conversation, allowing knowledge to be co-constructed through interaction.

Instructional Design Hierarchy for Chemistry Education

In education, people often use the terms teaching approach, teaching method, teaching strategies, and teaching techniques interchangeably, or they do not know what the terms actually mean. Actually, the terms describe different levels of instructional planning, each having a specific role in teaching and learning. A teaching approach refers to the overarching philosophy or belief system that shapes how instruction is designed and delivered. It reflects assumptions about how students learn best and serves as the foundation for selecting appropriate methods, strategies, and techniques.

Teaching approaches are commonly categorized as either teacher-centered or student-centered. In a teacher-centered approach, the teacher is the primary source of knowledge, often using structured methods like direct instruction and emphasizing content delivery and discipline. In contrast, a student-centered approach emphasizes active learning, collaboration, and the development of critical thinking skills through methods such as collaborative learning, inquiry-based learning, problem-based learning, and experiential learning (Killen, 2016). For example, a student-centered approach grounded in constructivist theory encourages learners to build their own understanding through exploration and reflection, whereas a teacher-centered approach influenced by behaviorist theory relies on repetition, reinforcement, and clear instructional cues. The chosen approach not only influences how the teacher interacts with students but also determines the overall learning experience and classroom environment. The next level of the instructional design is the teaching method.

A teaching method encompasses the principles, pedagogy, and management strategies that the teacher uses in the classroom (Sherma, 2023). Basically, the teaching method is the manner in which the teacher uses various strategies for the students to learn what is being taught. Teaching methods are systematic and guided by step-by-step instructions. The teaching method the teacher uses should be influenced by the teacher's educational philosophy, classroom demographics, subject area, and school mission statement. For example, in a chemistry classroom, a teacher who adopts an inquiry-based approach may guide students through a structured lab investigation in which they explore the effect of temperature on reaction rates by forming hypotheses, conducting experiments, and drawing conclusions under teacher supervision.

The most practical level of instructional design is the teaching technique, which refers to the specific classroom action or activity used to implement broader strategies and methods. According to Kumar (2022), teaching techniques such as streaming video, drama, model making, and educational games are effective tools that make learning more interactive, engaging, and accessible for students. In a chemistry classroom, a teacher might use model-making to help students visualize atomic structure or apply drama techniques to simulate particle collisions in gas laws. These hands-on activities transform abstract content into tangible experiences that support deeper understanding. Teaching techniques play a critical role in translating theoretical strategies into meaningful and practical learning outcomes.

Level	**Definition**	**Examples**
Teaching Approach	The broadest level. It reflects the educator's overall belief about how learning occurs, often categorized as teacher-centered or student-centered.	Teacher-Centered, Student-Centered
Teaching Method	A systematic way of implementing the teaching approach. It provides an overall plan for delivering instruction.	Inquiry-Based Learning, Direct Instruction, Experiential Learning, Conceptual Teaching
Teaching Strategy	A planned procedure for organizing and delivering content within a chosen method. Strategies guide the flow and interaction of instruction.	Active Learning, Case Study, Cooperative Learning, Discussion, Problem Solving, Small Group Work
Teaching Technique	A specific instructional activity or tool used during a lesson to support the strategy. It is the most	Demonstration, Brainstorming, Concept Mapping, Exit Ticket, Role Play

Level	Definition	Examples
	concrete level of classroom practice.	

Table 2.2: Hierarchy of Instructional Design: Teaching Approach, Method, Strategy, and Technique

In education, as shown by Table 2.2, the instructional design process operates across four hierarchical levels: teaching approach, method, strategy, and technique. At the highest level, the teaching approach reflects the teacher's beliefs about how students learn, often categorized as teacher-centered or student-centered, and is influenced by learning theories such as behaviorism or constructivism. This belief guides the selection of a teaching method, such as direct instruction for teacher- centered learning or inquiry-based learning for student-centered environments. A teaching strategy is then used to implement the method effectively, with common examples including active learning, case study, cooperative learning, direct instruction, discussion, problem solving, and small group work. Finally, the teaching technique refers to the specific classroom activity or tool used during instruction, such as demonstration, brainstorming, or concept mapping.

Examples of Instructional Design

Combustion of Ethanol, $C_2H_5OH + O_2 \rightarrow CO_2 + H_2O$

Teaching Approach (*Student-Centered – Constructivist*)

→ The teacher believes that students learn best by actively engaging with real-world phenomena.

- *What's happening:* The teacher designs a lesson where students explore a combustion reaction themselves rather than being told everything up front.

Teaching Method (*Experiential Learning*)

→ Students learn through direct observation and participation in a real chemical event.

- *What's happening:* Students watch the teacher ignite ethanol and observe flame colour, heat, and condensation forming.

Teaching Strategy (*Demonstration-Based Inquiry*)
→ The teacher uses a structured demonstration and asks students to make predictions, observe carefully, and explain outcomes.

- *What's happening:* Before the demo, the teacher asks, "What products do you expect when ethanol burns?" After the demo, students discuss evidence of water and carbon dioxide.

Teaching Technique (*Live Demonstration*)
→ A specific activity is used during the lesson to show the concept in action.

- *What's happening:* The teacher burns ethanol in a crucible, captures water on a cold surface (condensation), and passes the gas through limewater to show it turns milky — confirming CO_2 is produced.

This breakdown shows how each level builds on the next:

- Approach drives your philosophy
- Method shapes your general instructional style
- Strategy plans how content is delivered
- Technique is what the student sees and does in the classroom

Educational Technology Uses in Chemistry Education

Technology is reshaping education and society. It has made it easy to communicate across the world instantly and at minimal cost. This has greatly increased networking, collaboration, and the sharing of information. In chemistry education, advancements such as social media have increased access to new findings and information, facilitating intellectual discourse in the field (American Chemical Society, n.d.). However, the need for information literacy is now much more significant, as students and teachers must differentiate between credible and false information, especially when conducting research for assignments and other academic activities.

The emergence of computerized assessments allows students to obtain immediate feedback, and other forms of computerized resources have enhanced the learning experience (American

Chemical Society, n.d.). Also, teachers, students, and parents can now communicate easily through platforms such as Facebook and WhatsApp. Additionally, the professional development of teachers has greatly advanced and benefited from technology through access to online webinars and communication with colleagues. Educational blogs and chemistry-related YouTube videos can also be accessed online (American Chemical Society, n.d.).

The practical component of chemistry has benefited from the integration of data collection instruments with computer systems (American Chemical Society, n.d.). For example, digital sensors are used to measure pH, pressure, and temperature. The data collected can be displayed by computer systems in various forms, such as graphs, and can even generate regression equations. Teachers can now share videos of experiments, apparatus, and lessons with students. At times, some experiments are too dangerous or expensive to conduct, and showing a video or doing the lab virtually is a suitable alternative that was not available to previous generations. PhET and Concord Consortium are examples of online resources with high-quality simulations that provide an alternative to hands-on classroom activities. These simulations generally investigate atomic-level phenomena using computer-generated models of molecular motion and interactions (American Chemical Society, n.d.). Educational technology, if used correctly, can facilitate student-centered instruction by enabling visualization of concepts, interactive learning, and even personalized instruction.

Examples of educational technology used in the chemistry classroom include cell phones, projectors, wireless internet access, interactive whiteboards, graphing calculators, laptop computers, tablets, simulations, molecular modeling tools, augmented reality (AR), virtual reality (VR), digital databases, gamification platforms, learning management systems, data analysis tools, and audiovisual materials. The purposes and uses of the various technologies are mentioned below; however, the list of uses is not exhaustive.

List of Educational Technology

1. Cell Phones
   - Purpose: Communication and access to educational apps.
   - Chemistry Use: Share images of lab setups and complete group assignments.
2. Projectors
   - Purpose: Display instructional content to the whole class.
   - Chemistry Use: Show reaction mechanism animations to explain organic processes.
3. Wireless Internet Access
   - Purpose: Enable connectivity for online research and tools.
   - Chemistry Use: Access online simulations and databases during classroom instruction.
4. Interactive Whiteboards
   - Purpose: Facilitate interactive visual teaching.
   - Chemistry Use: Annotate molecular structures and balance equations collaboratively.
5. Graphing Calculators
   - Purpose: Solve and plot mathematical functions.
   - Chemistry Use: Plot graphs of the rate of reaction data for different concentrations.
6. Laptop Computers
   - Purpose: General-purpose computing and educational software access.
   - Chemistry Use: Analyze titration data using graphing and spreadsheet tools.
7. Tablets
   - Purpose: Portable access to apps, readings, and simulations.
   - Chemistry Use: Run simulations for molecular interactions or solution behavior.
8. Simulations
   - Purpose: Model processes and experiments virtually.
   - Chemistry Use: Simulate acid-base titrations or changes in gas laws under different conditions.
9. Molecular Modeling Tools

- Purpose: Visualize and manipulate molecular structures.
- Chemistry Use: Show 3D molecular geometry and bond angles.

10. Augmented Reality (AR)
    - Purpose: Overlay digital content onto real-world views.
    - Chemistry Use: Explore atomic models and compound structures in 3D space.
11. Virtual Reality (VR)
    - Purpose: Create immersive learning environments.
    - Chemistry Use: Perform virtual chemistry experiments in a simulated lab setting.
12. Digital Databases
    - Purpose: Provide access to research articles and chemical data.
    - Chemistry Use: Retrieve molecular properties, reaction data, or spectra.
13. Gamification Platforms
    - Purpose: Increase motivation through game-like learning.
    - Chemistry Use: Review periodic trends or chemical formulas through interactive games.
14. Learning Management Systems (LMS)
    - Purpose: Organize and deliver course materials and assessments.
    - Chemistry Use: Upload lab reports, conduct quizzes, and manage class resources.
15. Data Analysis Tools
    - Purpose: Interpret and visualize experimental data.
    - Chemistry Use: Generate graphs for titration results or compare reaction times.
16. Audio-visual Materials
    - Purpose: Support auditory and visual learning.
    - Chemistry Use: View tutorials on lab techniques or watch animated reaction mechanisms.

Classroom Management for Chemistry Educators

The classroom is a fluid place, constantly changing due to students' influence on each other, the teacher's influence on students, and students' influence on the teacher. Some of the most challenging encounters during classes include disruptions from talking, unruly students or class clowns, personality differences that fuel disagreements, struggles for dominance among students, and overcrowding, which negatively affects participation. It is important for students to consider the fact that each individual is unique, and there can be various reasons for bad behavior, such as homelessness, domestic violence, child neglect, poor socio-economic background, and linguistic barriers (GCU Blog, 2024).

Seven (7) Classroom Management Strategies (GCU Blog, 2024):

- The educator's expectations of students must be clear: Students must know that you respect them, and they should respect you and one another. Also, discuss with students their own expectations and explain how the class will benefit them throughout their lives, rather than simply emphasizing rules.
- Hold students accountable for their learning: Reinforce that students are responsible for their own academic progress. This encourages greater participation and makes them easier to teach.
- Do not shout: Always speak in a calm, normal tone during class, regardless of the situation. Students who are genuinely interested in learning will often help by asking others to remain quiet.
- Provide parents with feedback: Contact parents to offer praise for students who are doing well or making commendable efforts. This also applies to students with behavioral challenges, but be careful to communicate constructively to avoid creating resentment or disengagement.

- Celebrate student accomplishments: Make students aware of rewards for positive behavior, on-time assignment submission, and proper grooming and hygiene.
- Encourage and support positive peer relationships: Get to know your students and promote healthy socialization within the classroom environment.
- List class rules clearly: Rules should be visibly displayed in the classroom. Involve students in creating the rules at the start of the term, and assure them that only those who break the rules will face consequences. Figure 2.6 illustrates a visually engaging classroom rules poster featuring cartoon-style elements and simplified language to enhance student understanding and foster a positive learning environment.

Figure 2.6: Poster Showing Some General Class Rules

In secondary chemistry classrooms, effective classroom management often relies on implementing proactive strategies that promote safety, engagement, and responsibility. For example, establishing clear laboratory routines at the beginning of the term is a proactive approach that reduces confusion and fosters consistent student behavior. Assigning specific roles, such as materials handler or data recorder, during lab activities helps structure group work and minimizes off-task behavior. Another proactive strategy is to use visual aids, such as lab safety posters and checklists, to reinforce expectations and procedures. Incorporating positive reinforcement, such as verbal praise or a points system, encourages students to follow directions and participate actively. These strategies not only prevent disruptions but also support a positive classroom climate that enhances learning. When proactive classroom management is applied thoughtfully, it aligns with the instructional goals of chemistry education and contributes to a safe and productive learning environment.

The Role of Learning Styles in Chemistry Education

The article by Çelikler (2020) emphasizes the pivotal role learning styles play in chemistry education, particularly through the lens of Kolb's Experiential Learning Theory. Learning styles influence how students acquire, process, and retain chemical knowledge, and recognizing these differences can enhance classroom effectiveness. A key distinction is made between chemistry students who focus on chemical theory, research, and industrial applications and chemistry education students who study both chemistry content and pedagogical methods to become secondary-level teachers. In the study, chemistry students predominantly exhibited assimilating and converging learning styles, suggesting a preference for theoretical understanding and practical problem-solving, while chemistry education students leaned more toward the converging style, which supports applied learning and instructional preparation. These findings indicate that instructional methods should be adapted to align with these distinct learning preferences to improve comprehension and engagement. The study recommends tailoring both teaching strategies and classroom environments to learners' characteristics to foster active involvement in chemistry education. Such alignment enhances academic outcomes and promotes a more inclusive, student-centered learning environment.

There are different learning styles framed in various models, such as the VARK model and Kolb's experiential learning styles. Kolb's experiential learning theory categorizes learners based on how they perceive and process experiences (Kolb, 1984), while the VARK model classifies learners by their preferred sensory modalities for receiving information (Fleming & Mills, 1992). The list of learning styles under the models mentioned is presented in a simplified form for better understanding.

VARK Learning Styles (Fleming's Model)

- Visual (Visual Learners) learns through images, diagrams, charts, and spatial understanding.
- Auditory (Auditory Learners) learns through listening, discussions, and verbal instructions.
- Reading/Writing (Reading/Writing Learners) learns through reading texts, writing notes, and using written materials.
- Kinesthetic (Kinesthetic Learners) learns best through hands-on activities, experiments, and real-life experiences.

Kolb's Experiential Learning Styles

- Diverging (Diverging Learners) prefers observing situations from multiple perspectives and enjoys brainstorming and gathering information.
- Assimilating (Assimilating Learners) favors abstract concepts, theoretical models, and logical reasoning.
- Converging (Converging Learners) excels at solving problems and applying ideas in practical situations.

- Accommodating (Accommodating Learners) learns through doing, experimentation, and by relying on intuition rather than logic.

Examples of Different Learning Styles in Chemistry Classroom

The following categorized list presents a synthesis of learning styles from the VARK and Kolb models, each accompanied by contextualized examples specific to chemistry education. These examples illustrate how instructional strategies can be tailored to accommodate diverse learner preferences, thereby enhancing student engagement and conceptual understanding in the chemistry classroom.

VARK Learning Styles in Chemistry Classroom

- Visual Learners: These learners prefer visual representations such as diagrams, charts, and spatial layouts to understand content.

In Chemistry: They comprehend reaction mechanisms and molecular structures better through colorful diagrams and molecular models.

- Auditory Learners: They learn most effectively through listening, discussion, and verbal explanation.

In Chemistry: They grasp concepts like acid-base theory by participating in teacher-led discussions and listening to verbal explanations.

- Reading/Writing Learners: These students process information through reading and writing tasks.

In Chemistry: They retain concepts like oxidation-reduction by reading textbooks and rewriting content in their own words.

- Kinesthetic Learners: They understand material best through movement, experimentation, and hands-on tasks.

In Chemistry: They learn effectively during lab work, such as mixing chemicals and observing reactions firsthand.

Kolb's Experiential Learning Styles in Chemistry Classroom

- Diverging Learners: These learners observe situations from multiple perspectives and enjoy group brainstorming and reflection.

In Chemistry: They participate in analyzing lab results and exploring alternative methods through group discussions.

- Assimilating Learners: They prefer abstract thinking and structured content with logical sequencing.

In Chemistry: They excel in understanding theoretical topics like stoichiometry through lectures and organized notes.

- Converging Learners: They focus on problem-solving and applying theory to practice.

In Chemistry: They apply knowledge by designing experiments to test solubility or reaction rates.

- Accommodating Learners: These students rely on intuition and active experimentation to learn.

In Chemistry: They gain understanding through hands-on lab activities like acid-base titrations using trial-and-error approaches.

Importance of Reflective Practices in Education

The practice of continuous self-examination and self-evaluation that educators engage in to be effective and improve their professional practices is called teacher reflection or teacher reflective practice (Shandomo, 2009). Teacher reflective practices result in critical reflection. Critical reflection is a process that enables adults to identify assumptions that direct their actions and to trace the origins of those actions from a historical and cultural perspective. This process should cause the teacher to question what those assumptions mean and to seek suitable alternatives for action. For example, this process allows teacher candidates to gain greater depth of knowledge about their teaching styles, which helps them challenge ineffective traditional practices and become more effective teachers (Shandomo, 2009).

Through critical reflection, teacher candidates are guided to examine their own beliefs and recognize the disparity between their worldviews and the cultural backgrounds of their students. Shandomo (2009) emphasizes that such reflection helps bridge cultural gaps, especially in urban schools where predominantly White, middle-class teacher candidates work with ethnically diverse students. This contextual approach ensures that teacher candidates do not merely report events but begin to think critically about how their actions affect student learning. Reflective journaling, goal-setting, and conferencing all support this development, encouraging future teachers to challenge inherited assumptions and improve their instructional effectiveness. The formative process of reflection enables educators to adapt and refine their practice over time by learning from experience and feedback. Ultimately, reflection becomes not only a formative but also a transformative process that fosters equity, growth, and lifelong learning.

In addition to supporting teacher growth and self-awareness, reflective practices equip educators to navigate the complexities of constantly evolving educational environments. Machost and Stains (2023) explain that classrooms are dynamic spaces shaped by shifting student demographics, emerging technologies, and changes in curriculum standards. Reflection serves as a stabilizing force, or "gyroscope," that helps teachers remain aligned with their core values and pedagogical goals amid these changes. By deliberately analyzing what works, what doesn't, and why, educators can respond with greater clarity and adaptability during uncertain or high-pressure moments. This proactive engagement with reflective practice enhances not only individual decision-making but also empowers teachers to advocate for equitable curricular and institutional changes that better support diverse learners.

Example of Teacher Reflection in a Chemistry Class

Following a lesson on chemical bonding, a chemistry teacher noted that students struggled with the concept of electronegativity differences and their relationship to bond type. Despite using diagrams and verbal explanations, many learners displayed confusion during independent practice. Upon reflection, the teacher recognized the abstract nature of the examples and resolved to incorporate hands-on molecular model kits in subsequent lessons. A mid-lesson formative check will also be added to assess understanding before advancing. This reflective adjustment is aimed at improving conceptual clarity and engagement.

Prompt	Response
Topic Taught	
What Went Well.	
What Challenges Occurred.	
Student Understanding (Evidence).	
What Would I Change Next Time?	
New Strategies or Tools to Try.	

Table 2.3: Reflection Template for Chemistry Lessons

Assessment and Evaluation in Education

Assessment and evaluation are essential processes in teaching and learning, though they serve distinct purposes within the educational system. Assessment refers to the systematic process of gathering data about students' knowledge, skills, attitudes, or beliefs to inform instruction and improve learning outcomes (California Department of Education, n.d.; Ghaicha, 2016). It is ongoing and learner-centered, often providing teachers and students with feedback during the learning process. Evaluation, on the other hand, involves interpreting the results of assessments to make judgments about student performance, instructional effectiveness, or program quality (Starr, 2014). While assessment answers the question "How are students learning?", evaluation seeks to determine "How well did they learn?" or "Was the instruction effective?" (SAGE Publications, n.d.).

Formative and summative assessments are two major types of assessment that differ in purpose, timing, and impact. Formative assessment is conducted during the instructional process to monitor student progress and provide immediate feedback that guides both teaching and learning. It emphasizes growth and adaptation. Summative assessment occurs at the end of an instructional period to evaluate what students have learned. It is used for certification, grading, and accountability. The differences can be illustrated as follows:

Formative Assessment Examples:

- Exit tickets
- Learning journals
- Peer and self-assessments
- Class discussions
- Quick quizzes

Summative Assessment Examples:

- End-of-term exams
- Final research projects
- Lab reports
- Standardized tests
- Portfolios

Formative assessment supports learning by identifying gaps and misconceptions early, allowing teachers to adjust their instruction accordingly. In contrast, summative assessment provides a final measure of achievement and is often used to make high-stakes decisions such as promotion or certification (Northern Illinois University Center for Innovative Teaching and Learning, 2012; Darling-Hammond & Adamson, 2014).

Feature	Formative Assessment	Summative Assessment
Timing	During learning	After learning
Purpose	To monitor progress and guide instruction	To evaluate achievement

Feedback	Frequent, descriptive, and immediate	Usually limited or not provided
Examples	Quizzes, exit tickets, class discussions	Final exams, standardized tests, end-of-unit projects
Impact on Learning	Improves ongoing learning	Judges overall learning
Used By	Teachers and students	Teachers, administrators, policymakers

Table 2.4: The Difference between Formative and Summative Assessment

Rubrics and feedback are crucial tools for enhancing the effectiveness of both formative and summative assessments. A rubric is a structured guide that defines clear performance criteria for a specific task, such as a science lab report or oral presentation (Cornell University Center for Teaching Innovation, n.d.). It helps ensure consistency and transparency in scoring. For example, a chemistry rubric might include the following categories: hypothesis formulation, experimental procedure, data accuracy, analysis, and presentation. Rubrics may be analytic, which break down performance into components, or holistic, which evaluate work as a whole. In both cases, descriptive feedback aligned with the rubric helps students reflect on their strengths and areas for improvement. Feedback plays a central role in formative assessment by supporting student self-regulation and motivation (Mamoon-Al-Bashir, Kabir, & Rahman, 2016).

The importance of assessment and evaluation lies in their ability to improve teaching practices, guide student learning, and support data-driven decisions in education. Assessment promotes active learning, supports differentiated instruction, and allows timely interventions. Evaluation, meanwhile, ensures accountability and informs policy or curricular revisions (Ghaicha, 2016). A thoughtful integration of both processes, through varied methods such as performance tasks, peer reviews, and digital assessments, enables educators to capture a comprehensive view of student achievement and instructional effectiveness. Understanding the difference between assessment and evaluation empowers teachers to purposefully design activities that support growth while also maintaining academic standards and expectations.

Example of Assessment in a Chemistry Classroom

During a lesson on chemical reactions, the teacher gives students a five-question quiz covering reaction types and equation balancing. This is a formative assessment intended to check understanding during instruction. The teacher reviews the quiz results with the class, explains common errors, and reteaches key concepts. This review is essential, as formative assessments must be discussed with students to support learning and guide improvement. Without such interaction, the assessment would not fulfill its formative function.

Example of Evaluation in a Chemistry Classroom

At the end of a unit on stoichiometry, students complete a lab report involving theoretical yield and limiting reactants. The teacher uses a rubric to assign a final grade. This is a summative evaluation used to certify achievement and inform report cards. In most cases, the report is graded and returned without discussion, as summative assessments are not typically reviewed with students. However, if the teacher later discusses common mistakes from the lab report to help students prepare for future work, it becomes a **summative-formative assessment**, which is a hybrid assessment, serving both evaluative and instructional purposes.

Example of Rubric Use in a Chemistry Classroom

To grade the stoichiometry lab report, the teacher uses the following simple rubric:

Criteria	Excellent (4 pts)	Good (3 pts)	Fair (2 pts)	Poor (1 pt)
Procedure Clarity	Steps clearly outlined and logical	Mostly clear, with minor omissions	Unclear or incomplete steps	Steps missing or confusing
Data Accuracy	All values correct and	Minor errors in	Several inaccuracies	Data mostly incorrect or

Criteria	Excellent (4 pts)	Good (3 pts)	Fair (2 pts)	Poor (1 pt)
	labeled	recording		missing
Calculations	All calculations correct with units	Minor calculation errors	Frequent mistakes	Incomplete or incorrect calculations
Conclusion Quality	Well-supported and insightful	Generally accurate	Basic or vague explanation	Incomplete or incorrect reasoning

Table 2.5

The rubric provides clear performance expectations and promotes fairness. It may be used purely for grading (summative) or discussed with students (formative), depending on instructional intent.

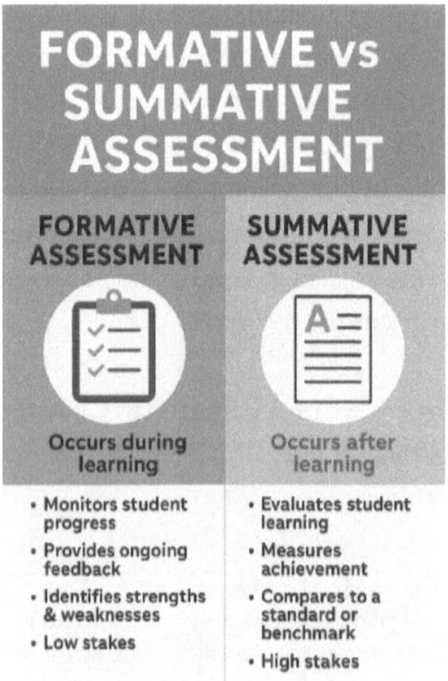

Figure 2.7: Comparing Formative and Summative Assessment

The Importance of Teacher Professional Development in Education

Initial teacher training is essential to obtain foundational knowledge as a teacher. However, continuous learning and development, in the form of professional development, are necessary to increase one's expertise and promote lifelong learning. Professional development is essential because teachers are now finding themselves in diverse classrooms where the students have different learning needs, academic performance levels, socio-economic backgrounds, and linguistic needs (OECD, n.d.-b). Therefore, teachers must use various innovative approaches relating to pedagogy and technology to help them attain the learning objectives. Additionally, teacher professional development helps improve teacher quality and supports teacher retention.

Organizations should provide incentives for teachers to continuously develop themselves as part of lifelong learning and to ensure they remain current with developments in education (OECD, n.d.-b). A teacher can continue their professional development through taking courses such as formal education courses, conferences, seminars, workshops, online training opportunities, and networking and sharing expertise among colleagues.

Many teachers face limited access to high-quality professional development due to budget constraints and a lack of institutional support. In some regions, professional development opportunities are not aligned with teachers' actual classroom challenges, reducing their practical value. Furthermore, the rapid evolution of educational technology requires teachers to continuously update their digital competencies to remain effective. Without ongoing support and feedback, professional development may become a one-time event rather than a sustained process of growth. There is also a need to address teacher burnout, which professional development can help mitigate by equipping teachers with stress management techniques and adaptive instructional strategies.

Examples of Teacher Professional in Chemistry Education

One initiative a chemistry teacher can take is to attend workshops on using virtual labs and simulations to enhance students' understanding of abstract chemical concepts. These may include training courses on tools like PhET Interactive Simulations and Chem Collective. Another initiative involves joining professional learning communities such as the Royal Society of Chemistry (RSC) and the American Chemical Society (ACS) to collaborate, share resources, and explore best practices in chemistry education. A third initiative is enrolling in online courses through platforms like Alison and edX, which offer training in both chemistry content and innovative teaching strategies.

The Future of Chemistry Education

The future of chemistry education at the secondary level is expected to be shaped by the increasing use of digital tools and the gradual introduction of data literacy concepts. While secondary students may not engage directly with advanced automation or machine learning, introducing basic chemical informatics and data interpretation through simulations and virtual labs can enhance conceptual understanding. ACD/Labs emphasizes that early exposure to such tools builds foundational skills that align with modern scientific practices and prepares students for post-secondary pathways in science and technology (ACD/Labs, n.d.). Resources such as PhET and ChemCollective are examples of accessible platforms that help students visualize complex chemistry topics, supporting active learning in secondary classrooms. However, effective implementation depends on teacher training and infrastructure support to ensure digital tools are used meaningfully and equitably.

In addition to technology integration, recent research emphasizes the importance of diverse teaching strategies that address students' individual learning needs and enhance classroom engagement. Blonder, Rap, and Mamlok-Naaman (2023) identify themes such as modeling, skill development, and personalized instruction as critical to advancing chemistry education. While much of this research originates in higher education, the principles are adaptable to secondary contexts when appropriately simplified and scaffolded. For example, using student-centered approaches and differentiated assessments can help address learning disparities and reduce anxiety in science classrooms. To ensure lasting impact, professional development for secondary teachers must be aligned with these strategies, enabling them to translate research-based methods into practical classroom applications.

Future trends in secondary chemistry education point toward greater integration of digital technologies, interdisciplinary learning, and career-oriented instruction. With the growing demand for skills in green chemistry, data science, and pharmaceutical research, educators are encouraged to align classroom learning with emerging scientific careers. This includes introducing students to real-world applications of chemistry through virtual labs, project-based learning, and career exploration modules. Emphasis is also being placed on sustainability and environmental science, reflecting global shifts toward climate-conscious industries. By aligning instruction with these trends, chemistry education can better prepare students for both advanced studies and the evolving science workforce.

Chapter 2
Methodology

This book employs a qualitative approach, using document analysis and a reflective-practitioner inquiry design, to examine the alignment of classroom instructional practices with established learning theories and preferred learning styles. The primary aim is to evaluate the instructional materials and class evaluations of selected course content gathered by a CSEC Chemistry teacher through the review of lesson plans, examinations, classroom evaluations, homework assignments, class activities, and other related materials. These materials will be assessed to identify strengths and weaknesses, favored learning theories, and preferred learning styles. The purpose of this analysis is to inform instructional improvements and to provide resources that support other teachers in analyzing and enhancing their instructional practices and teaching materials.

Research Approach

This research adopts a qualitative approach to explore instructional practices through non-numerical analysis. It uses document analysis to examine lesson plans, evaluations, assignments, and other instructional materials. A reflective-practitioner inquiry design is employed to critically assess the alignment of these materials with learning theories and preferred learning styles.

Sample

The sample consists of selected instructional materials and class evaluations accumulated over time by an educator. These include lesson plans, assessments, homework assignments, classroom activities, and formal evaluation reports from a CSEC Chemistry classroom.

Ethical Consideration

Ethical considerations for this book focus on the use of instructional materials while safeguarding confidentiality. The research is limited to studying materials such as lesson plans, student homework, class evaluations, and examinations. Although these materials originate from a school where an anonymous educator is employed, no student names or school identifiers will be disclosed.

Data Analysis Procedure

This book follows a two-part qualitative procedure using (1) the READ approach for document analysis and (2) a reflective-practitioner inquiry model. The READ model provides a clear and structured method for reviewing instructional documents, while the reflective-practitioner inquiry guides critical evaluation through systematic reflection on instructional practices (Schön, 1983).

Part 1: Document Analysis Procedure (READ Approach)

Adapted from the READ model (Solomon, 2024):

- Ready your materials: Collect instructional materials, including lesson plans, class evaluations, student homework, classroom activities, and examinations.
- Extract data: Review each document, noting the type of document, content, learning activities, and assessments to better understand the nature of each item.
- Analyze data: Examine each document for alignment with specific learning theories and learning styles. Relevant strengths and weaknesses will also be identified.
- Distill findings: Identify instructional strengths and weaknesses, dominant learning theories, and the learning styles most supported. Summarized insights will inform recommendations for pedagogical improvement.

Part 2: Reflective-Practitioner Inquiry Procedure

Based on Schön (1983), reflective-practitioner inquiry will proceed in three steps:

- Observation: Review the instructional documents as static representations of teaching practice, noting teaching goals and expected student outcomes.
- Reflection-in-action: Simulate real-time reflection by considering how instructional choices might have supported or hindered student learning, based on learning theories and cognitive models.
- Reflection-on-action: Engage in post-review analysis to draw conclusions about teaching effectiveness, identify gaps, and recommend adjustments or enhancements to better support diverse learners.

Chapter 3

Data Analysis, Findings and Improvements

This section incorporates the experiences of an educator who has been teaching CSEC Chemistry along with other subjects. It involves the analysis of instructional materials to examine the educator's teaching practices, with a focus on identifying strengths, weaknesses, and areas for improvement. The review considers how these practices align with established learning theories, preferred learning styles, and pedagogical standards. Particular attention is given to respecting the specific requirements and expectations associated with teaching CSEC Chemistry. The reflections drawn from this analysis aim to support instructional refinement and enhance the overall quality of teaching and learning.

Class Evaluation/Reflection Analysis

Class evaluation is a reflective tool that enables teachers to systematically document the activities and dynamics of a lesson. It captures key aspects, including student behavior, learning outcomes, instructional successes, and challenges in lesson delivery. Through this process, teachers can identify areas of concern, highlight aspects needing improvement, and assess the overall effectiveness of their teaching strategies. Additionally, class evaluations provide teachers with space to express their thoughts, feelings, and professional judgments about what worked and what did not. It also allows teachers to share their emotional responses to the lesson; however, such reflections should be approached with caution to ensure they remain constructive and professional.

Class Evaluation Sample 1

Evaluation October 2-6, 2023

The week was similar to the previous one. The students are making the teaching process difficult. However, the lessons continue to progress according to the lesson plans. Grade 10A and Grade 10B have conducted two labs to fulfil the SBA requirement for CSEC Chemistry. They continue with the *States of Matter* lesson plan. Grade 7 HFLE examined factors affecting adolescent development, and the teacher conducted an interview to assess students' knowledge and explain the factors. The students were marked based on their oral responses, clarity, and tone when they spoke. Grade 11B and Grade 11A have basically completed the topic of Energetics. Grade 11B did not attend class on October 6, 2023; otherwise, they would have completed the topic as well.

Evaluation October 9-13, 2023

The students' general behavior leaves much to be desired. The classes for the week were activity-based for Grade 7 Science to prepare them for the six-week test. Grade 10A's behavior is still not acceptable; however, the topic *States of Matter* was completed. Grade 10B, a much smaller class, also misbehaved but managed to complete the same topic. Grade 7 HFLE involved randomly selecting articles from reputable sources. The teacher read the articles aloud to the class, omitting any inappropriate content. This effectively explored the factors affecting adolescent development. The Grade 11 classes completed the topic of *Energetics*. Various teaching techniques were used to educate students, including lectures (presentations), article reviews, experiments, demonstrations, and quizzes. Grade 7 Science also conducted a demonstration using sodium thiosulfate and hydrochloric acid to learn how to make scientific observations.

Class Evaluation–Sample 2
Class: Grade 10A
Subject: Chemistry
Date: May 19, 2025

Summary:
The Chemistry lesson on mole concepts was delivered clearly and effectively. The teacher maintained a good standard of instruction as usual.

However, student behavior during the lesson was not satisfactory and did not meet expected standards. This affected the overall classroom environment.

Conclusion:
The lesson itself was well taught, but improvement in student malicious behaviour is needed to support better learning outcomes.

Class: 7 Science
Subject: Integrated Science
Date: May 19, 2025

Summary:
The lesson on *Energy Forms and Interconversion*, including renewable and non-renewable energy sources, was delivered as planned.

While a few students participated and asked questions, overall behavior was poor, with some students creating conflict. The teacher was not pleased with the apparent and disruptive behavior.

Conclusion:
The lesson objectives were met, but the students' malicious behavior must stop to maintain a positive learning environment.

Class: 7 HFLE
Subject: HFLE
Date: May 19, 2025

Summary:
The lesson covered the topic *Enough to Eat*, focusing on food security and food insecurity. Students also learned about ways to achieve food security.

The class misbehaved and showed disregard for the teacher. However, the teacher maintained professionalism throughout the session.

Conclusion:
The lesson was delivered as planned. Students' malicious behaviour must stop to ensure a respectful and productive learning environment.

Class Evaluation/Reflection Findings

This chapter presents the findings from a document-based analysis and reflective-practitioner inquiry into weekly class evaluations conducted across multiple grades and subjects. The purpose was to assess instructional practices, evaluate behavioral dynamics, and determine alignment with educational theory and diverse learning styles. A total of 15 weekly evaluations, dated between September 9, 2023, and May 30, 2025, were reviewed.

General Standards for Class Evaluation

The evaluations generally met the core expectations of classroom assessment documentation. Each entry provided a clear record of the subject, class, date, and topics covered. For example, in the October 2–6, 2023 evaluation, it was noted: "Grade 10A and Grade 10B have conducted two labs to fulfil the SBA requirement for CSEC Chemistry." This indicates lesson pacing is maintained despite classroom challenges. Pacing refers to how instruction aligns with scheduled plans and curriculum timing, and in this case, lessons continued to follow the intended progression.

Lesson objectives were typically referenced, either explicitly or implicitly, through summary descriptions of activities. However, some evaluations lacked direct mention of assessment feedback or differentiated instruction. These omissions highlight an area where the evaluations can be strengthened for greater diagnostic value.

Emotional Reflection and Professionalism

Emotional expressions appeared consistently in the evaluations, reflecting the teacher's candid perspective. Frustration with student behavior is a common theme, seen in phrases like "student behavior during the lesson was not satisfactory" (May 19, 2025) and "students' general behavior leaves much to be desired" (October 9–13, 2023). At the same time, the teacher maintained a tone of professionalism, stating in one entry, "the teacher maintained professionalism throughout the session" (May 19, 2025).

While emotions were present, they were generally used to contextualize challenges rather than to assign blame. Nonetheless, future evaluations would benefit from balancing emotional reflection with pedagogical analysis to ensure reflective growth.

Instructional Strengths and Weaknesses

A consistent strength across the documents was lesson continuity. Despite behavioral issues, lessons such as "States of Matter," "Energy Forms and Interconversion," and "Food Security" were delivered as planned. The use of practical strategies—including lab work, article readings, and oral assessments—demonstrates the teacher's commitment to active learning. In the October 9–13, 2023 evaluation, a demonstration using sodium thiosulfate and hydrochloric acid was described, showing alignment with experiential learning models.

On the other hand, the most frequent weakness reported was disruptive or malicious student behavior. For example, the entry for Grade 7 HFLE on May 19, 2025, stated: "The class misbehaved and showed disregard for the teacher." Behavioral issues were especially prevalent in lower grades (e.g., Grade 7 and Grade 10A) and were repeatedly cited as impediments to effective teaching. This highlights the need for classroom management interventions and differentiated behavior strategies.

Recommendations for Improvement

Improvements to the class evaluation process should focus more on student learning outcomes rather than just behavior. Few evaluations referenced how well students understood the content or responded to instruction. Including specific feedback on assessment performance or formative checks would strengthen the evaluations.

Instructionally, behavior issues suggest a need for varied engagement strategies and perhaps more structured routines. In addition, some reflections lack self-critique regarding teaching effectiveness, such as questioning whether lesson methods were accessible to all learners or whether adjustments were made in response to classroom dynamics.

Learning Theories and Learning Styles

The instructional practices described align with several learning theories. Constructivist approaches are evident in student-centered discussions and experiments. For example, in the November 20–24, 2023 entry, the HFLE class "focused on having an engaging discussion" about mental health, a strategy grounded in social constructivism.

Behaviorist elements were evident in the use of questioning, direct instruction, and oral assessments, as in the interview conducted during the October 2–6 HFLE lesson. Cognitive learning theory is reflected in the use of diagrams and article reviews to support content comprehension.

Learning styles catered to include visual (e.g., textbook diagrams, drawings of atomic structure), auditory (e.g., oral responses and article readings), and kinesthetic (e.g., lab work and demonstrations).

These practices demonstrate a balanced effort to engage diverse learners, though evaluations rarely included evidence of how students with different learning preferences performed.

Conclusion of Class Evaluation/Reflection Analysis

The analysis shows that while the evaluations reflect instructional dedication and structure, they would benefit from deeper pedagogical reflection and more specific learning outcome analysis. For instance, few evaluations provided insight into how instructional strategies were adjusted in response to student misunderstandings or whether alternative methods were considered for students who struggled. A deeper pedagogical reflection would involve analyzing not just what was taught, but how and why certain strategies were chosen, and whether they effectively supported diverse learners. For example, instead of simply noting that "a lab was conducted," the evaluation could reflect on how the lab contributed to conceptual understanding of the mole concept or whether students demonstrated improvement in scientific reasoning.

Similarly, a more specific learning outcome analysis would include data- or observation-based judgments of student achievement. Rather than stating that a lesson was "completed," evaluations could note whether students met the intended objectives, such as calculating moles from mass, or whether reteaching or reinforcement was required. This would strengthen the evaluations as formative tools for instructional improvement.

Classroom behavior was a recurring challenge, but lessons were generally completed with fidelity. In particular, the Chemistry instruction for Grade 10A and Grade 10B demonstrated consistent alignment with lesson pacing and curriculum expectations, including laboratory sessions to meet SBA requirements and completion of core topics such as *States of Matter* and *Mole Concepts*. Despite behavioral disruptions, especially in Grade 10A, the evaluations revealed a sustained effort to maintain instructional progress and fulfil CSEC Chemistry standards.

There is clear evidence of alignment with multiple learning theories, including constructivism, behaviorism, and cognitive theory, as well as with learning styles such as visual, auditory, and kinesthetic. These were demonstrated through student discussions, oral assessments, hands-on experiments, and visual aids. However, more intentional documentation of student responses and differentiated practices would enhance the overall instructional reflection process.

New Template for Class Evaluation and Reflection

Class Evaluation and Reflection Template	
Section	**Details**
Class	
Subject	
Date	
Topic	
Objectives Covered	
Lesson Delivery Summary	
Student Engagement and Behaviour	
Teaching Strategies Used	
Assessment and Feedback	
Strengths Observed	
Areas for Improvement	
Reflections (Emotional & Professional)	
Learning Theory Alignment	
Learning Styles Addressed	
Follow-up Actions	

Table 4.1: Template for Conducting Class Evaluation and Reflection

Section Explanations

- Class: Indicate the grade or group (e.g., Grade 10A, Grade 7 Science).

- Subject: Specify the subject taught (e.g., Chemistry, HELE)
- Date: Record the date of the lesson.
- Topic: State the specific topic or concept addressed (e.g., Mole Concept, States of Matter).
- Objectives Covered: List the intended learning outcomes or instructional goals.
- Lesson Delivery Summary: Describe how the lesson was implemented. Indicate whether it followed the lesson plan and note any adjustments or pacing concerns.
- Student Engagement and Behavior: Comment on students' level of participation, collaboration, attentiveness, and any behavior issues observed.
- Teaching Strategies Used: Outline the instructional methods used, such as experiments, lectures, discussions, role-plays, or visual aids.
- Assessment and Feedback: Describe how students were assessed (formative/summative) and what kind of feedback was provided during or after the lesson.
- Strengths Observed: Highlight what worked well in the lesson delivery (e.g., student interaction, clarity of concept, engagement).
- Areas for Improvement: Identify aspects that need change or development for future lessons (e.g., time management, resource use, differentiation).
- Reflections (Emotional & Professional): Share emotional insights (e.g., frustration, satisfaction) and professional judgment regarding the success or challenges of the lesson.
- Learning Theory Alignment: Indicate which educational theory best fits the lesson approach (e.g., constructivism, behaviorism) and briefly explain why.
- Learning Styles Addressed: Mention which learner preferences were considered (e.g., visual through diagrams, kinesthetic through labs, auditory via discussion).
- Follow-up Actions: Suggest specific steps to address challenges or build on strengths for the next lesson.

Lesson Plans and Assessment Analysis

A lesson plan is a written guide that supports the structured delivery of instruction in the classroom. It outlines what the teacher intends to teach, how it will be taught, the resources needed, and how student learning will be assessed. Lesson plans are typically developed using established learning theories such as constructivism, behaviorism, and cognitivism, which provide frameworks for understanding how students acquire knowledge. Additionally, lesson planning takes into account different learning styles, such as visual, auditory, and kinesthetic, to ensure all students are engaged and supported. One effective model used in planning is the 5E instructional approach, which includes the stages Engage, Explore, Explain, Elaborate, and Evaluate; this model encourages inquiry-based learning and helps students build knowledge through observation, hands-on experiences, discussion, application, and assessment.

The 5E lesson plan model includes five stages that support active learning. Engage sparks interest and connects to prior knowledge. Explore allows students to investigate through hands-on activities. Explain involves sharing findings and introducing key concepts. Elaborate extends understanding through application. Evaluate checks for comprehension through assessment and reflection.

Lesson Plan Sample 1

Mixture and Separation Lesson Plan	
Name	
Date	February 17, 2025
Subject Area	Chemistry
Grade Level	10
Duration	6 hours
Short Description	The substances we use in our day-to-day lives are usually mixtures. This lesson will enable students to be able to distinguish them from each other, understand their properties and how

	to separate them using different techniques.
Lesson Summary	Matter is anything that has mass and occupies space. Mass is simply the quantity or amount of matter that a substance contains. We use a balance to measure the mass of an object. Matter can be classified into two main groups: pure substance and mixture. A pure substance can either be an element or a compound while a mixture is either homogeneous or heterogeneous. 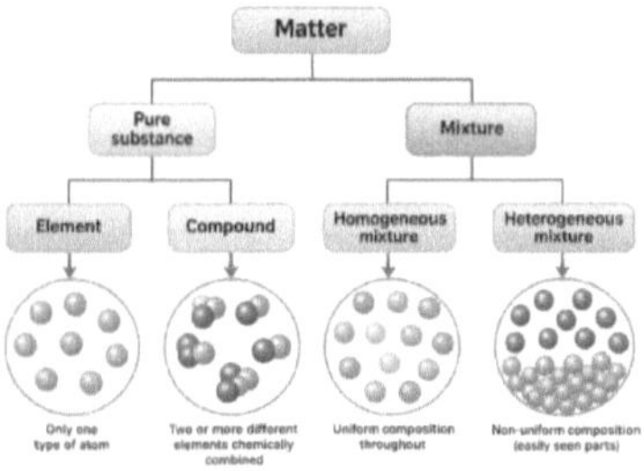 A solution is a homogeneous mixture of one or more solutes dissolved in a solvent. The major component of a solution is the solvent, and the minor component is known as the solute. A colloid is a heterogeneous mixture in which the dispersed particles are intermediate in size between those of a solution and a suspension. Solubility is the amount of that substance that is required to form a saturated solution in a given amount of solvent at a specified temperature. Solubility of solute in a solution is determined by structure of the solute and solvent, and the temperature. Substances commonly occur as mixtures. Therefore, it is essential to know how to separate mixtures. The separation Technique used is determined by the different substance physical properties. Examples of separating techniques are filtration, evaporation, simple distillation, separating funnel, solvent extraction, and chromatography.

Specific Objectives	• Mixture and Separation distinguish between pure substances and mixtures. • Distinguish among solutions, suspensions and colloids. • Identify different types of solutions. • Investigate the effect of temperature on solubility of solids in water. • Apply suitable separation techniques based on differences in properties of the components of mixtures. • Describe the extraction of sucrose from sugar cane.
Real World Connections or Applications	• A lot of products such as drinks, value-added food, and medicine are mixtures of various substances in a particular ratio or percentage composition. • Sodas, smoke, paint, alloys. Some of the substances we use every day are mixtures and those will give a hands-on perception to the topic.
Link to National Development Goals	• **Goal 1** Jamaicans are empowered to achieve their fullest potential. Quality science education is important for driving research and development in any country. Therefore, quality STEM education at high school is necessary for smooth transition into university. • **Goal 2** Jamaica's economy is prosperous- Knowledge of mixture and separation is essential for mining and manufacturing. Obtaining aluminum from bauxite and sugar from sugar cane are examples. The bauxite and sugar industries are major foreign exchange earner for Jamaica.
Vocabulary	• Mixture, homogeneous, heterogeneous, solution, suspension, colloid, extraction, filtration, chromatography, evaporation, separating funnel, simple distillation, and fractional distillation
Materials	• Handouts, laptop, audio-visual material

Expected Prior Knowledge		
Lesson Outline	**Teacher**	**Student**
Engagement	The lesson will commence with a discussion about mixtures and game. The game will involve identifying mixtures.	Students will identify the images or words as either mixture or pure substance.
Exploration	The teacher will do a demonstration by making different mixtures. The students will actually get to make the different mixtures under the teacher supervision.	Students will state whether the respective mixture is heterogeneous or homogeneous.
Explanation	The teacher will conduct a mini-lecture to cover the CSEC syllabus. For instance, explain in detail what are solution, suspension, and colloid. And, list and explain the separation methods.	The students should name at least four separation techniques before teacher begins.
Elaboration	Teacher utilizes videos to reinforce lesson and highlight industrial uses of separating techniques.	The teacher will give the students the opportunity to go to the board and name some product made using separating techniques.
Evaluation	The students will be evaluated using homework, a class quiz, and an online quiz. Other assessment methods may be used.	The students should score 50% and above in order to pass the evaluations.

Assessment	Class activity – 10 marks Homework – 10 marks Online quiz – 10 marks
Handouts	Class activity
Links & Resources including websites	Solution – https://www.youtube.com/watch?v=Pn8P-QtJQH4 Suspension – https://www.youtube.com/watch?v=hWGgDakuUNc Colloid – https://www.youtube.com/watch?v=QAH-cCK1bS8 Separation Techniques https://www.youtube.com/watch?v=YfkAzAx2j0A Extraction of Sugar: Short & animated https://www.youtube.com/watch?v=ce4ESoqtgnk Long and detailed https://www.youtube.com/watch?v=q40M2yNCJQg
Learning Outcomes	Students should be able to: • Define a pure substance • Compare boiling point of pure and impure substances • Define a mixture • List the types of mixtures and examples • Define a solution • Identify the different types of solutions • Explain the composition of the different types of solutions • Define suspension • Define colloids • Define solubility and perform solubility calculations • List and explain the types of separation techniques • Draw the apparatus used for filtration, simple distillation, fractional

	distillation, and separating funnel • Explain the process of extracting sucrose form sugarcane
Skills and Interrelationship	• Biology- solutions in life processes • Biology- transport system • Biology- function of the kidney and digestive system • Physics- gas laws, circular motion, and specific latent heat (sugar cane)

Table 4.2

Lesson Plan Sample 2

Mole Concept Lesson Plan	
Name	
Date	May 8, 2025
Subject Area	Chemistry
Grade Level	10
Duration	8 hr
Short Description	This lesson defines mole, molar mass, relative molecular mass, formula mass, and atomic mass. Also, this lesson teaches students how to calculate moles, the number of particles, and percentage composition.
Lesson Summary	The mole is a unit of measurement similar to a pair, a dozen, and a gross. A mole of substance is said to contain Avogadro's number (Avogadro's constant) of particles. The value of Avogadro's constant is 6.023×10^{23}. A mole is defined as the amount of substance (Avogadro's number of atoms, molecules, and ions). The mole ratio of a balanced chemical equation can be used to calculate the amount of an unknown reactant or product once the mole (mass) of one reactant is known.
Specific Objectives	• Define mole and molar mass • Perform calculations involving the mole • State Avogadro's Law • State the Law of Conservation of

Mole Concept Lesson Plan		
	Matter • Write balanced equations	
Real World Connections or Applications	• In everyday life, the mole concept is essential, especially when it comes to cooking, manufacturing medications, and combating environmental pollution. It is useful for determining pollution levels, guaranteeing that medicine dosages are proper, and precisely measuring ingredients in recipes.	
Link to National Development Goals	• Jamaicans are empowered to achieve their fullest potential: Jamaica needs skilled people who can tackle environmental issues and can prepare the medication for citizens to ensure a healthy and stable population. Also, knowledge about mole concepts is essential for world-class chemistry education. • Jamaica's economy is prosperous: the ability to calculate the amount of reactants and products is essential for manufacturing, especially those involving chemical reactions.	
Vocabulary	Avogadro's constant, atomic mass, mass, molar mass, mole, relative molecular mass	
Materials	Text books, calculators, computer, markers, sample worksheet, white board	
Expected Prior Knowledge		
Lesson Outline	**Teacher**	**Student**
Engagement	The teacher will ask students to name common units of measurement.	The students are expected to mention dozen, pair, and gross as unit of measurements.
Exploration	The teacher will state the mole of any substance as a particular mass	The students must identify that the mass number (atomic mass), formula mass and

Mole Concept Lesson Plan		
	and contain Avogadro's number of particles.	molecular mass of substance are equal to one mole of the substances.
Explanation	The teacher will conduct a lecture to explain the mole concept.	The students will take notes and are expected to ask questions.
Elaboration	The teacher will facilitate students performing mole calculation and percentage composition.	The students will conduct the calculations in groups.
Evaluation	The students will be evaluated using homework, a class quiz, and an online quiz.	The students should score 50% or above in order to pass the evaluations.
Assessment	Class activity – 10 marks Homework – 10 marks Online quiz – 10 marks	
Handouts	Notes and practice questions	
Links & Resources including websites	What is titration and how it is performed: https://www.youtube.com/watch?v=YqfvRBJ-iPg Titration curves and acid-base indicators: https://www.youtube.com/watch?v=1YlXtpF-19A Indicators: https://www.youtube.com/watch?v=62-RLhY9gXU Preparing a standard solution: https://www.youtube.com/watch?v=iPYyRNjXkgY Percent composition by mass: https://www.youtube.com/watch?v=lywmGCfIUIA	
Learning Outcomes	Students should be able to: • Define mole, molar mass, formula mass and molecular mass. • State Avogadro's constant, 6.023×10^{23}.	

Mole Concept Lesson Plan	
	• Perform calculations involving mole. • Perform percentage composition calculation to determine the abundance of elements in a compound. • Calculate the relative molecular mass and relative formula mass given atomic masses (mass number). • Distinguish between relative masses and molar masses. • Calculate moles and volume of gas using molar volume at room temperature and pressure (r.t.p) and standard temperature and pressure (s.t.p). • State the law of conversation of matter.
Skills and Interrelationship	Physics – Kinetic theory

Table 4.3

Assessment Samples

Organic Chemistry Homework

1. Give four characteristics of a homologous series. (4 marks)
2. Draw the functional group for the following organic compounds.
    a. Alcohol (1 mark)
    b. Alkane (1 mark)
    c. Alkene (1 mark)
    d. Alkyne (1 mark)
    e. Carboxylic acid (2 marks)

Metals Class Activity

a. Why do metals have high melting points and boiling points?

b. Why do metals have high density?
c. What are the general names for salts produced from reacting reactive metals with either hydrochloric acid or sulfuric acid?

Acids, Bases, and Salts Class Activity

- Define the terms base, alkali, and amphoteric substance.
- Write a balanced chemical equation for the reaction of the following:
  - The reaction between magnesium hydroxide and nitric acid.
  - The reaction between calcium oxide and ammonium nitrate.
- Calcium oxide is a basic oxide. Explain, using a chemical equation, why calcium oxide is basic.

Structure and Bonding Class Activity

1. Objective (5 minutes): Students will work in groups of 5 to draw dot-and-cross diagrams for different compounds, identify the type of bonding, and present their work to the class.
2. Peer Review (5 minutes): The students will have five minutes to help struggling classmates.
3. Class Presentation (5 minutes): Ten students selected randomly present their diagrams to the class. The teacher corrects any misconceptions and reinforces key learning points.
4. Teacher (10 minutes): The groups will visit the teacher's desk, and their work will be graded.

Structure and Bonding – One-Minute Reflection

1. Objective: To assess your understanding of key concepts related to atomic structure and chemical bonding.
2. Instructions for Students: You will have one minute to explain what you have learned so far about structure and

bonding. You may choose to do this as either a short-spoken response (individual or recorded) or a written paragraph no longer than 100 words.

General Rubric – One-Minute Reflection (Total: five Marks)

Criteria	Marks
1. Informative and relevant	
The response clearly focuses on structure and bonding concepts.	2 mark
2. Use of scientific terms	
Correct use of key vocabulary (e.g., atom, electron, ionic, covalent).	1 mark
3. Scientific accuracy	
The explanation contains accurate facts and correct descriptions.	1 mark
4. Clarity and structure	
Ideas are logically organized and easy to understand.	1 mark

Table 4.4

Lesson Plan and Assessment Findings

This section presents a document-based analysis of selected Chemistry lesson plans and associated assessments using the READ approach and reflective-practitioner inquiry. The focus is on evaluating instructional structure, alignment with learning theories and styles, assessment practices, and pedagogical strengths and weaknesses. The lesson plans analyzed include topics such as Mixtures and Separation, Atomic Structure, Mole Concept, Acids and Bases, Electrochemistry, Energetics, Metals, and Green Chemistry. Assessment tools reviewed include homework assignments, in-class activities, one-minute reflections, and drawing tasks.

General Structure and Pacing

The lesson plans follow a consistent two-week instructional cycle, totaling six hours, including one hour for laboratory activities. Most plans demonstrate well structured pacing aligned with this model. For example, the "Mixtures and Separation" lesson plan outlines progressive activities over multiple sessions with time allocations that include introductory engagement, exploration, and consolidation activities. This organization reflects deliberate pacing to allow for knowledge-building and hands-on application.

The plans generally align with the 5E instructional model. The "Engage" phase is commonly executed through warm-up activities or guiding questions. "Explore" activities involve demonstrations or lab-based learning, such as the filtration activity in the "Mixtures and Separation" lesson. "Explain" phases include teacher-led discussions, while "Elaborate" tasks are achieved through homework and group-based application. "Evaluate" stages appear in the form of end-of-lesson questioning, quizzes, or student reflections.

Instructional Strengths and Weaknesses

A key strength observed is the integration of active learning strategies. Lessons use diverse formats, including games (e.g., "Bonding Battle"), student presentations, and lab activities to support conceptual development. For example, the "Atomic Structure" plan incorporates drawing atomic models, which engages visual and kinesthetic learners. The "Mole Concept" lesson includes real-world examples and problem-solving exercises that reinforce numeracy and logical reasoning.

However, some lesson plans lack explicit differentiation strategies for varying learner abilities. While some plans provide scaffolding through questioning, many do not indicate accommodations for students who may struggle with complex content. Additionally, transitions between lesson phases are sometimes underdeveloped, potentially affecting lesson flow and continuity.

Use of Learning Theories and Learning Styles

The lesson plans reflect a blend of constructivist, behaviorist, and cognitive approaches. Constructivist strategies are evident in inquiry-based activities and collaborative problem-solving. For example, the "Green Chemistry" lesson encourages students to evaluate real-world environmental practices. Behaviorist elements emerge in the use of direct instruction, drills, and immediate feedback on practice problems. Cognitive theory is represented through concept mapping and visual aids like atomic structure diagrams.

In terms of learning styles, the lessons address visual learners through diagrams and videos, auditory learners through discussions and teacher explanations, and kinesthetic learners through lab experiments and model-building activities. The varied strategies demonstrate planning to cater to diverse student needs, though some could further emphasize multimodal reinforcement.

Assessment Practices

A variety of assessments were used to monitor student learning. Homework assignments, such as those for "Acids and Bases" and "Mixtures and Separation," contain structured practice and challenge problems. Class activities involve critical thinking tasks and group collaboration. Of particular note are the one-minute reflections and drawing assessments introduced in recent lessons.

The "One-Minute Reflection on Bonding" asks students to briefly describe what they learned and identify unclear areas. This metacognitive task supports formative assessment by encouraging self-evaluation. Drawing assessments, such as those used in the "Atomic Structure" topic, allow students to visually represent abstract concepts, providing insight into their comprehension. These forms of assessment are aligned with best practices in formative evaluation and reflective learning.

Recommendations for Improvement

To further enhance the lesson plans, greater emphasis should be placed on differentiated instruction. Including alternative tasks or tiered activities would support learners at varying proficiency levels. Additionally, assessment criteria could be more explicitly aligned with learning objectives to allow for more targeted feedback. Incorporating student voice and peer assessment strategies could also strengthen engagement and ownership of learning.

Finally, lesson transitions and time allocations should be more clearly defined to ensure smoother lesson delivery and better time management.

Conclusion for Lesson Plan and Assessment Analysis

The Chemistry lesson plans and assessments demonstrate a comprehensive and thoughtful approach to instructional design, particularly in the context of CSEC Chemistry. The incorporation of the 5E instructional model provides a logical and pedagogically sound framework for lesson delivery. For example, the "Mixtures and Separation" lesson begins with an engaging discussion on everyday examples of mixtures, followed by a filtration experiment, and concludes with class discussion and homework. This structure supports conceptual understanding and mirrors the natural flow of inquiry-based science learning.

Assessment tools are especially commendable for their variety and depth. The use of one-minute reflections allows students to reflect on what they have learned and identify areas of confusion, thereby promoting metacognitive awareness. Drawing tasks, such as those used in the "Atomic Structure" lesson, offer visual and kinesthetic learners the opportunity to show their understanding of electron shells and atomic models in a creative and diagnostic manner. These tools serve as both reflective practices and formative assessments.

The lesson plans also show intentional alignment with learning theories. Constructivist elements are evident in group work, student inquiry, and real-world problem-solving, such as the environmental analysis in the "Green Chemistry" lesson. Cognitive theory is used through sequencing, concept building, and the integration of visual aids, while behaviorist strategies appear in direct instruction and guided practice exercises.

Despite these strengths, there is a need for more consistent differentiation across lesson plans. Some topics lack clear support for diverse learners, and transitions between phases of the lesson are occasionally abrupt. Incorporating strategies like tiered questioning or flexible groupings would enhance inclusivity and ensure that all students can access the content.

In summary, the Chemistry lesson plans reflect a balanced, learner-centered design supported by effective assessment tools and sound theoretical foundations. When implemented with more targeted differentiation and clearer instructional transitions, these lessons have strong potential to improve student outcomes in CSEC Chemistry and to model best practices in science education.

Improvement to Lesson Plan and Assessments

Teachers often struggle to complete the CSEC Chemistry syllabus, and the variety of assessments used is frequently limited. Syllabus adaptation is one approach that can help address this challenge by reorganizing how and when content is taught. It involves prioritizing critical and more complex concepts for in-depth coverage during class time. Therefore, simpler or lower-weighted objectives can be assigned for independent learning, or less class time can be allocated to their discussion. For example, essential theories or SBA-related skills can be taught through guided instruction, whereas basic definitions or straightforward objectives can be addressed through homework, online quizzes, or brief five-minute reviews supported by short notes and at least one example. Additionally, teachers should diversify assessments by including puzzles, diagram labeling, and scaffolded questions.

Scaffolded questions might prove to be particularly helpful for teaching students how to solve multi-step problems that involve calculations, such as mole concept calculations. Syllabus adaptation has the potential to make the CSEC Chemistry syllabus more manageable and accessible to students by enhancing diversity. However, SBA reports must be written in accordance with the official guidelines provided by CXC or the relevant examination body. Additionally, create a **rubric** for each assessment to ensure consistent marking and fairness.

Example of an Improved Lesson Plan

Syllabus adaptation will be used to develop the lesson plan for the CSEC Chemistry topic of the mole concept. Syllabus adaptation is being used to diversify the instructional activities to the extent possible. However, any requirements stipulated by the examination will be strictly adhered to, because that is the point where attempts to diversify truly end. The hope is that successes from using syllabus adaptation will then influence changes to the CSEC subjects syllabus. The starting point for syllabus adaptation to cater to diverse learners and to improve pedagogy is to align lesson plans, assessments, tests, examinations, and practicals (lab activities) with the syllabus objectives and requirements. Also, to identify major and minor concepts, the teacher should review official examinations to see which questions usually carry the most marks and which concepts students find most difficult.

Most of the guided instruction time in class should be dedicated to those major concepts when teaching their respective topics. For example, mole calculation is a major challenge or is difficult to learn for most students. This means most of the guided instruction or teaching time in class should focus on doing mole calculations. Minor concepts are those that are easier to learn or can be learned independently without teacher guidance. For example, learning about indicators and examples of indicators. However, it is recommended that two to five minutes of discussion should occur in class on minor concepts using examples and short notes, such as two sentences of explanation or one standard PowerPoint slide of information.

Major concepts for a topic might require at least three slides to adequately cover the concepts, using at least three examples and a minimum of two sentences of notes for each slide. In other words, thirty (30) minutes or more of guided instructions would be required for students to learn the concept or skill being taught. For example, it might take twenty (20) minutes using an example to explain graphing and providing notes. Then, the students are supported by the teacher to do an example over another twenty-minute period, and finally, the students do a similar example independently in groups of four or five in twenty minutes, which the teacher will grade and return to the students. The teacher will review the graded work with the students and assign three graphing questions for homework, which might require the teacher at least 20 minutes. Therefore, teaching graphing to an adequate level would have taken at least 1 hour and 20 minutes of directed interaction with the teacher. This structure supports modeling (teacher demonstrates), scaffolding (teacher assists), collaborative learning, and independent practice and assessment.

The nature of the classroom is fluid, which means teaching graphing will most likely take more than 1 hour and 20 minutes, but having a tight timeline prevents time-wasting. The 1 hour and 20 minutes should not double to teach the skill or require fifty (50) percent more time. Preparing the class material and having a lesson flow chart will help prevent this from happening. Remember, you cannot wait until all students master a concept or skill to move on when preparing students for external examinations, such as CSEC, because the syllabus will not be completed. The school or teacher having a past paper revision class where at least ten past papers are reviewed should help address that problem, and the students' independent studying using past papers, notes, graded assessments, and video, especially based on past papers for the examination, such as CSEC Chemistry past papers solution videos on YouTube.

Another major issue to consider when you are a teacher is the need to avoid plagiarism. There are many online databases with multiple-choice questions, structured questions, puzzles, and more. Teachers often use those resources without modification, which, honestly, constitutes plagiarism. It is recommended that teachers use questions from sources that allow free usage of their materials without requiring permission or licensing fees. Also, questions can be modified by slightly changing the wording, replacing substances with similar ones, and changing certain values. Artificial Intelligence (AI) can easily modify materials, making the task less intimidating.

Mole Concept Lesson

Lesson	Major Concepts	Minor Concepts
Lesson 1: Mole Foundations *(5 hours)*	-Mole calculations - Writing and balancing chemical equations - Calculating relative molecular and molar mass - Applying Avogadro's Law - Molar volume at r.t.p and s.t.p	- Define mole and molar mass - Percentage composition - Unit conversion (e.g., g → kg)
Lesson 2: Volumetric Analysis *(4 hours, incl. 1-hour lab)*	- Molar and mass concentration calculations - Balanced molecular and ionic equations - Titration apparatus and procedure	- Define standard solution - Preparing standard solutions - Indicators - pH scale

Table 4.5: Major and Minor Concept Table for Mole Concept Lessons

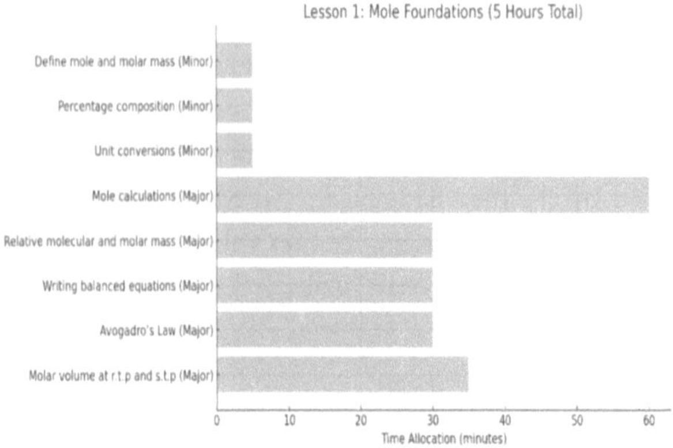

Figure 4.1: Mole Concept Lesson 1 Progression and Time Allocations

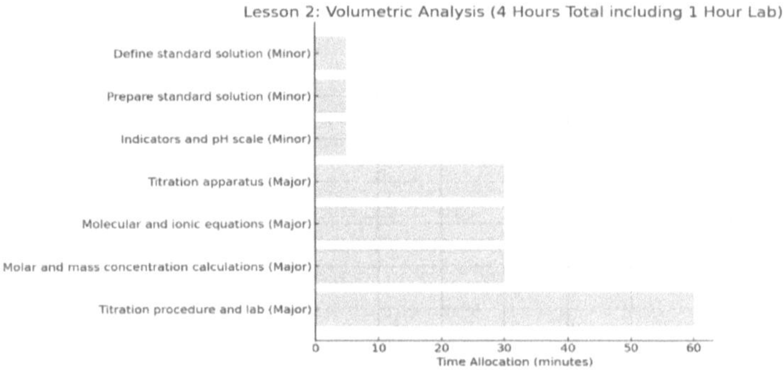

Figure 4.2: Mole Concept Lesson 2 Progression and Time Allocations

Lesson Flow Chart or Lesson Progression

Lesson 1: Mole Foundations (5 Hours, No Lab)

- Define mole and molar mass (Minor) – 5 minutes
- Percentage composition (Minor) – 5 minutes
- Unit conversions (Minor) – 5 minutes
- Mole calculations (Major) – 60 minutes
- Relative molecular and molar mass (Major) – 30 minutes
- Writing balanced equations (Major) – 30 minutes
- Avogadro's Law (Major) – 30 minutes

- Molar volume at r.t.p and s.t.p (Major) – 35 minutes

Lesson 1: Mole Foundations spans five hours and introduces both foundational and advanced mole concepts. The lesson begins with minor concepts such as defining mole and molar mass, percentage composition, and unit conversions, each covered in 5 minutes. It then progresses to major concepts including mole calculations (60 minutes), relative molecular and molar mass (30 minutes), writing balanced equations (30 minutes), Avogadro's Law (30 minutes), and molar volume at room temperature (r.t.p) and standard temperature and pressure (s.t.p) (35 minutes). The sequence is based on the CSEC Chemistry textbook and PowerPoint notes to build conceptual understanding logically.

Lesson 2: Volumetric Analysis (4 Hours, Includes 1-Hour Lab)

- Define standard solution (Minor) – 5 minutes
- Prepare standard solution (Minor) – 5 minutes
- Indicators and pH scale (Minor) – 5 minutes
- Titration apparatus (Major) – 30 minutes
- Molecular and ionic equations (Major) – 30 minutes
- Molar and mass concentration calculations (Major) – 60 minutes
- Titration procedure and lab (Major) – 60 minutes

Lesson 2: Volumetric Analysis, a four-hour session including a one-hour lab, begins with brief introductions to standard solutions, indicators, and the pH scale, each taught in 5 minutes. The lesson emphasizes titration apparatus (30 minutes), molecular and ionic equations (30 minutes), and molar and mass concentration calculations (60 minutes). It culminates in a detailed 60-minute laboratory exercise on titration procedures. This structure ensures that students have a theoretical grounding before engaging in hands-on analysis, aligning with multimodal learning strategies and the 5E instructional model. The progression supports both cognitive understanding and practical application, allowing students to engage through visual (diagrams, written equations), auditory (teacher explanation, peer discussion), and kinesthetic (lab work, drawing tasks) learning styles. Both lessons are intentionally sequenced to build from simple definitions to complex problem-solving, providing scaffolding and ensuring students are well-prepared for the CSEC Chemistry assessments.

Mole Concept: Mole Foundations Lesson Plan	
Teacher name	
Date	
Subject Area	Chemistry
Grade Level	
Duration	5 hours
Short Description	• This lesson introduces the mole concept, including mole calculations from mass, Avogadro's constant, and relative molecular mass, and molar volume calculations. It also emphasizes writing balanced equations and understanding the Law of Conservation of Matter.
Lesson Summary	• The mole is a unit of measurement similar to a pair, a dozen, and a gross. A mole of substance is said to contain Avogadro's number (Avogadro's constant) of particles. The value of Avogadro's constant is 6.023×10^{23}. A mole is defined as the amount of substance (Avogadro's number of atoms, molecules, and ions). • The mole ratio of a balanced chemical equation can be used to calculate the amount of an unknown reactant or product once the mole (mass) of one reactant is known.
Specific Objectives	• Define mole and molar mass • Perform mole calculations • Calculate relative molecular and molar mass

Mole Concept: Mole Foundations Lesson Plan	
	• Write balanced chemical equations • State Avogadro's Law • Perform gas volume calculations at r.t.p. and s.t.p
Real-World Connections	• Understanding the mole is essential for medication dosing, measuring environmental pollutants, and food science. Students will use real-life data from food containers and everyday chemical products to perform calculations, helping them connect abstract concepts to real applications.
Link to National Development Goals	• A sound grasp of chemistry enables students to address environmental challenges and contribute to public health. Mole concepts support national goals related to scientific literacy, pharmaceutical competence, and sustainable industrial development in Jamaica.
Vocabulary	• Avogadro's constant, atomic mass, molar mass, mole, relative molecular mass, molar volume, conservation of matter
Materials	• Textbooks, calculators, whiteboard, handouts, food packaging, sugar samples, measuring cylinders, digital scale
Expected Prior Knowledge	• Students should be familiar with atomic structure, simple chemical formulas, and basic algebraic manipulation.
5E Model - Engagement	• Students are randomly asked to name everyday grouping units (pair, dozen, gross). They would have already research assigned parts of the mole concept topic before the lesson and give 30-

Mole Concept: Mole Foundations Lesson Plan	
	second summaries at random at the start of the class.
5E Model - Exploration	• The teacher introduces Avogadro's number and asks students to compare it with quantities such as a dozen and gross. Students work in pairs to calculate the mole of sugar or salt based on real food labels.
5E Model - Explanation	• A teacher-led discussion clarifies how to calculate moles from mass and derive molar and molecular masses. The Law of Conservation of Matter and balanced equations are introduced here.
5E Model - Elaboration	• Students engage in scaffolded problem-solving tasks for mole calculations, gas volumes, and balanced equations. In groups, they identify the mole ratios in sample reactions.
5E Model - Evaluation	• Students complete homework involving mass-to-mole conversions and balancing equations. They also participate in a quiz and submit online responses. Exit tickets will include one calculation and a reflection prompt.
Assessment	• Class Activity: Scaffolded questions on mole calculations (10 marks) • Homework: Balancing equations (10 marks) • Online Quiz (10 marks) • Exit Ticket and One-Minute Reflection (Formative)
Handouts	• Summary notes on mole foundations, guided examples, and practice questions

Mole Concept: Mole Foundations Lesson Plan	
Links & Resources including websites	• Provide links to sites and YouTube videos here.
Learning Outcomes	Students should be able to: • Define mole, molar mass, formula mass and molecular mass. • Perform mole calculations from mass • Calculate percentage composition • Distinguish between relative molecular and molar mass • State and apply Avogadro's Law • Calculate molar volume of gases at r.t.p. and s.t.p.
Skills and Interrelationship	• - Physics: Kinetic Theory

Table 4.6

This lesson plan integrates multiple learning styles and learning theories to ensure inclusive and effective instruction. Visual learners benefit from diagrams, videos, and drawing tasks used to illustrate concepts such as molecular structure and molar relationships. Auditory learners engage through oral presentations, peer-to-peer discussions, and teacher explanations that reinforce understanding through listening. Kinesthetic learners are supported through hands-on demonstrations, such as calculating moles using real sugar samples and analyzing food labels to find the mass of the substances and to calculate the mole of the substances. From a theoretical perspective, constructivism is evident in student-led research and peer sharing activities, which allow learners to construct meaning through exploration and collaborative dialogue. Cognitive theory underpins the use of scaffolded problem-solving tasks, mental modeling strategies, and sequenced guided notes to support memory retention and conceptual clarity. Finally, behaviorist principles are applied through formative assessments and immediate feedback from quizzes and class discussions, reinforcing correct responses and encouraging continuous improvement.

<table>
<tr><th colspan="2">Mole Concept:
Volumetric Analysis or Titrimetric Analysis Lesson Plan</th></tr>
<tr><td>Teacher name</td><td></td></tr>
<tr><td>Date</td><td></td></tr>
<tr><td>Subject Area</td><td>Chemistry</td></tr>
<tr><td>Grade Level</td><td></td></tr>
<tr><td>Duration</td><td>4 hours</td></tr>
<tr><td>Short Description</td><td><ul><li>This lesson introduces students to volumetric analysis focusing on molar and mass concentration calculations, titration techniques, and solution preparation. Students will conduct a titration to determine the molar concentration of sulfuric acid using sodium hydroxide as the standard solution.</li></ul></td></tr>
<tr><td>Lesson Summary</td><td><ul><li>Chemical analysis plays an important role in the book of the composition or constituents of substances or materials. Chemical analysis is broadly divided into two types:<ul><li>Qualitative analysis</li><li>Quantitative analysis.</li></ul></li><li>Volumetric analysis is also known as titrimetric analysis. Titration involves measuring a volume of a solution of known concentration (titrant) that is required to react quantitatively with another solution of unknown concentration (analyte).</li></ul></td></tr>
<tr><td>Specific Objectives</td><td><ul><li>Perform molar and mass concentration calculations</li><li>Write ionic and molecular equations</li><li>Identify titration apparatus and state their functions</li><li>Define and prepare standard solutions</li><li>Understand indicators and the pH scale</li><li>Conduct titration and interpret data</li></ul></td></tr>
</table>

Mole Concept: Volumetric Analysis or Titrimetric Analysis Lesson Plan	
Real-World Connections	• Volumetric analysis or titrimetric analysis is used in the food industry to measure additives like salt and vitamins accurately. In pharmaceuticals, it ensures the purity and correct concentration of medicines, which often contain substances in varying amounts.
Link to National Development Goals	• This lesson aligns with Jamaica's scientific development goals by fostering analytical skills and laboratory competence crucial for careers in health, manufacturing, and environmental science.
Vocabulary	• Titration, molar concentration, mass concentration, standard solution, indicator, pH scale, equivalence point, burette, pipette, conical flask
Materials	• Titration setup (burette, pipette, conical flask, stand), standard NaOH, unknown H_2SO_4, indicators, beakers, white tiles, calculators, data sheets
Expected Prior Knowledge	• Students should be familiar with calculating molar mass and molar volume, and using mole ratios derived from balanced chemical equations.
5E Model - Engagement	• The teacher will begin by recapping key content from the previous lesson, focusing on mole ratios. To connect learning with real-world relevance, students will be asked to find the concentration of alcohol in popular beverages using provided data, sparking interest and curiosity.
5E Model - Exploration	• Students examine titration apparatus and match functions to each part. They practice setting up the equipment under teacher supervision.
5E Model - Explanation	• Teacher explains concentration formulas and demonstrates titration. Students record observations, learn proper reading of burette and use indicators.
5E Model - Elaboration	• Students perform a full titration. They calculate molar and mass concentrations,

Mole Concept: Volumetric Analysis or Titrimetric Analysis Lesson Plan	
	compare results, and analyze the experiment's relevance. The lab report will be written according to the CSEC Chemistry SBA requirements.
5E Model - Evaluation	• Exit tickets require students to solve one concentration problem and reflect on lab experience. Homework includes writing balanced ionic equations and identifying apparatus.
Assessment	• Lab Performance and Report (20 marks) • Homework (10 marks) • Online quiz on concentration calculations (10 marks) • Exit ticket and one-minute reflection (formative)
Handouts	• Summary notes on volumetric analysis, guided examples, and practice questions
Links & Resources including websites	• Provide links to sites and YouTube videos here.
Learning Outcomes	Students should be able to: • Calculate molar and mass concentrations • Accurately set up and use titration apparatus • Draw and label the titration apparatus • Write balanced molecular and ionic equations • Define primary and secondary standards • Prepare and describe standard solutions • Interpret pH and indicator data • Name indicators and their color change
Skills and Interrelationship	

Table 4.7

The Volumetric Analysis lesson plan applies a range of learning theories and learning styles to support deep understanding and accommodate diverse learners. From a constructivist perspective, the lesson allows students to actively build knowledge through lab investigations, such as preparing and analyzing standard solutions during titration. They learn by doing, making connections between theory and practice. Cognitive learning theory is applied through scaffolded calculations, progressive problem sets, and conceptual sequencing, from defining molarity to executing full titration calculations. This approach strengthens mental modeling and aids in long-term retention. Behaviorist theory is reflected in the use of immediate feedback through quizzes, oral responses, and guided correction of titration steps, reinforcing correct procedures and promoting consistent habits.

In terms of learning styles, visual learners benefit from labeled diagrams of titration apparatus, color-coded pH indicators, and reaction equations. Auditory learners engage through teacher-led explanations, group discussions, and oral presentation of results. Kinesthetic learners are supported through hands-on lab activities, including solution preparation, titration techniques, and real-time observation of color changes at endpoints. Read/write learners interact with structured worksheets, lab reports, and stepwise procedural notes. The combination of these strategies ensures an inclusive classroom environment that fosters both conceptual mastery and practical skill development in chemistry.

Mole Concept Assessments

Assessment 1 Class Activity: Scaffold Mole Concept Question with Partial Solution

Calcium hydrogencarbonate reacts with nitric acid as follows:

$Ca(HCO_3)_2(s) + 2HCl(aq) \rightarrow CaCl_2(aq) + 2CO_2(g) + 2H_2O(l)$

A student adds 7.5 g of calcium hydrogencarbonate to excess hydrochloric acid.

i. Calculate the number of moles of calcium hydrogencarbonate used.

Use the formula:

$n = m / M_r$

Given:

- $m = 7.5$ g
- M_r = ________

$n = 7.5$ / ________ = 0.05 mol

(2 marks)

ii. Determine the number of moles of carbon dioxide produced.

From the equation:

1 mol $Ca(HCO_3)_2 \rightarrow$ 2 mol CO_2

$n(CO_2) = 2 \times$ ________ = 0.1 mol

(2 marks)

iii. Calculate the volume of carbon dioxide produced at r.t.p.

Use the formula:

Volume = n × molar volume

Molar volume = 24 $dm^3\ mol^{-1}$

Volume = ________ × 24 = 2.4 dm^3

(2 marks)

Rubric Class Activity	
Criteria	**Marks**
Correctly identified all missing values	3 marks
Correct molar mass (Mr) calculation	3 marks

Table 4.8

Assessment 2 Homework: Labeling Titration Apparatus

Instruction: Label the titration apparatus and state the purpose of each part. (8 marks)

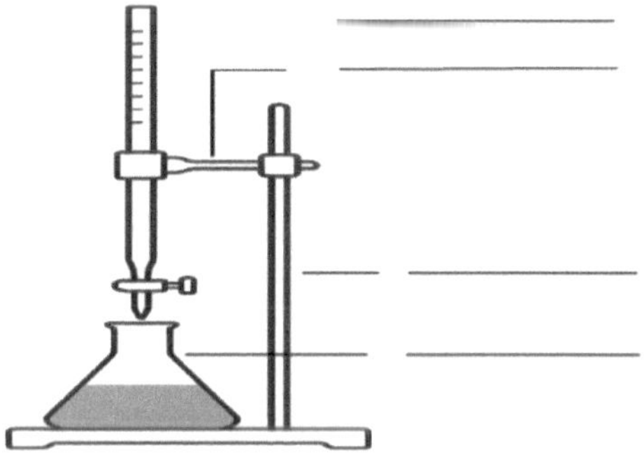

Figure 4.3

Rubric: Titration Apparatus Labeling (Total: 8 Marks)	
Criteria	**Marks**
Correctly labeled 4 parts of the apparatus	4 marks (1 mark each)
Accurately stated the purpose of each part	4 marks (1 mark each)

Table 4.9

For assessments that use diagrams and charts, each should include a clear title and be supported by at least 2 explanatory sentences that demonstrate student understanding. However, some diagrams and charts should not be accompanied by explanatory sentences, such as scientific drawings and drawings of experimental apparatus, unless specifically and expressively required. Labeling should be used where necessary to identify important features. This approach aligns with visual and read/write learning styles, allowing students to process information more effectively. From a cognitive theory perspective, combining visual representation with written explanation reduces cognitive overload and reinforces mental models. Reinforcing mental models occurs as students integrate visual and verbal elements into coherent frameworks using visual anchoring, which helps them retain and retrieve information by linking concepts to specific visual cues. Chunking information into labeled parts also makes complex processes easier to follow and simulate mentally. Constructivist learning principles are also applied as students build and demonstrate understanding by connecting visual data to scientific concepts. This method not only supports content mastery but also encourages critical thinking and clearer communication in scientific assessments.

Class Instruction Analysis

This section analyzes the instructional materials used in class, with a focus on notes given in class and PowerPoint presentations. It explores how visuals, such as crystallization sketches, are integrated into these materials to support conceptual understanding. The section also reflects on the strengths and limitations of using these resources in classrooms with limited access to digital technology.

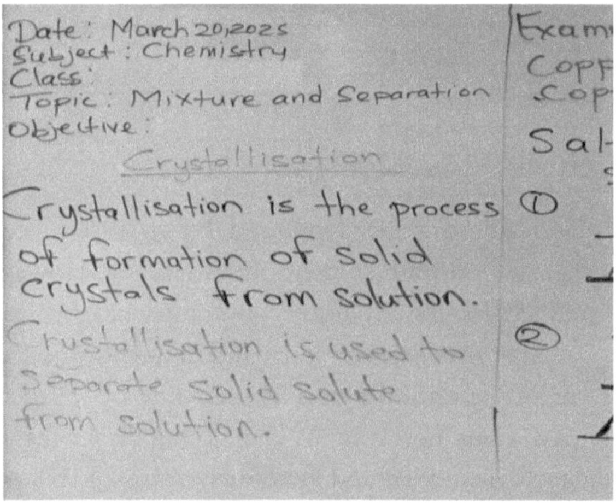

Figure 4.4: Evidence of Instruction in Classroom 1

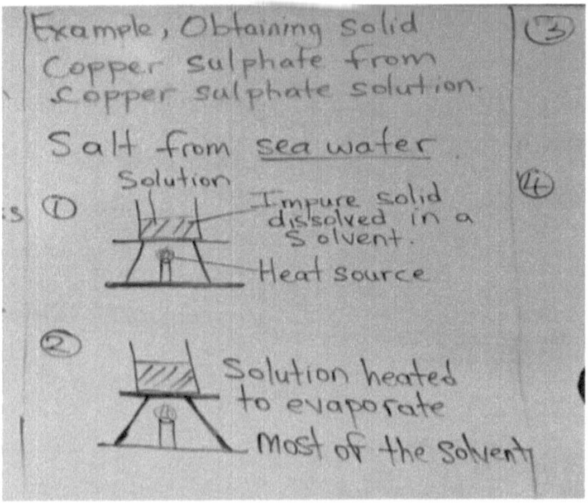

Figure 4.5: Evidence of Instruction in Classroom 2

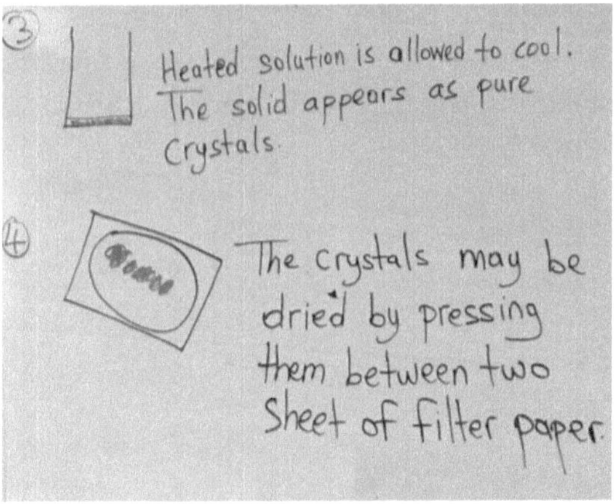

Figure 4.6: Evidence of Instruction in Classroom 3

This section evaluates the use of instructional materials, specifically class notes, that were used to teach crystallization and separation techniques. Figures 13, 14, and 15 illustrate various stages of the process, such as heating a solution, filtration, evaporation, and crystal formation. These visuals were produced by the teacher to compensate for limited access to digital tools such as smartboards or projectors. They align with the CSEC Chemistry curriculum by visually reinforcing practical laboratory setups and fundamental processes in separation. The diagrams aid student understanding through clearly sequenced steps and simplified representations, though labels and directional arrows could be added for clarity and accuracy.

From a pedagogical standpoint, these visuals support several learning theories. The diagrams serve as cognitive anchors that enhance visual learning and reduce mental overload by chunking information. They also reflect constructivist principles, allowing students to interpret or replicate the drawings, thereby constructing their own understanding of each process. The behaviorist model is also supported through the repeated use and practice of drawing and labeling diagrams. Sharing pictures and videos via WhatsApp is a good alternative if access to digital technology is limited. Hand-drawn diagrams have been a staple in classrooms for centuries. Therefore, access to technology must not replace drawing diagrams by hand completely in a classroom. Even smartboards can facilitate drawing by hand, preserving this important instructional practice.

Figure 4.7: Sample of Notes -1

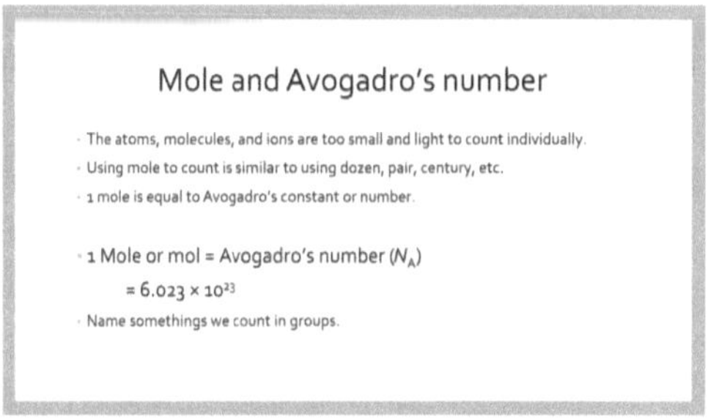

Figure 4.8: Sample of Notes -2

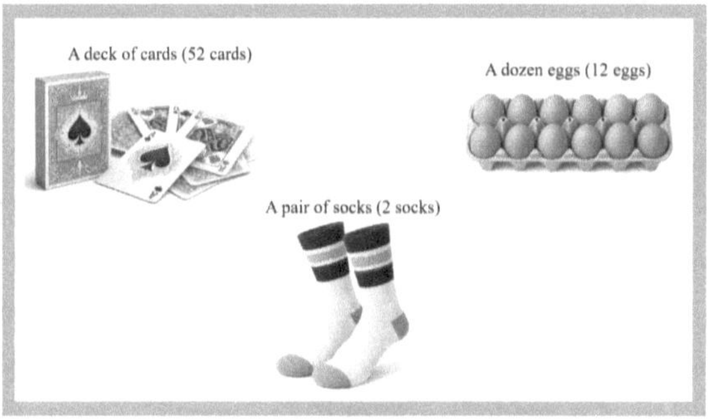

Figure 4.9: Sample of Notes -3

The PowerPoint notes used in the Chemistry classroom reflect a structured, syllabus-aligned approach to teaching CSEC topics (see figures 16, 17, and 18). Topics such as acids and bases, atomic structure, electrochemistry, and mixtures are presented using slides that include clear headings, definitions, examples, and chemical equations. Visual aids such as labeled diagrams, flowcharts, and tables are consistently used to simplify complex processes, such as electrolysis and the composition of atoms. These features help reduce cognitive overload and enhance understanding, especially for visual learners. However, while the notes are clear and content-rich, some slides can be improved with more color contrast, iconography, and spacing for better readability. Additionally, brief application-based questions or real-life images can be embedded to increase engagement and contextual relevance. YouTube links are often provided alongside the notes to reinforce key concepts outside of class.

Pedagogically, the notes demonstrate a cognitive learning orientation, using sequencing and scaffolded examples to guide students from basic recall to application-level thinking. Constructivist learning is supported when students engage with these materials during discussion or problem-solving sessions, and when they take notes directly from the presentations. From a learning styles perspective, the PowerPoint slides cater primarily to visual and read/write learners through diagrams and structured text. However, including auditory or interactive elements, such as simulations or voice-over explanations, can expand accessibility for diverse learners.

Mid-term and Final Examination Analysis

The final examination is designed to closely mirror the structure and style of the external CSEC Chemistry examination. As such, no significant effort is made to diversify or alter the format in a unique way. It is strongly recommended that internal final exams replicate the external format, consisting of two papers: a multiple-choice paper and a structured response paper. However, the exam should only assess topics that have been covered in class. In contrast, the mid-term test offers greater flexibility for diversification, though it is advisable to ensure that at least 50 percent of the questions resemble those on the external exam, which imposes no restrictions. To enrich the mid-term experience, additional formats such as puzzles, fill-in-the-blank questions, true/false statements, essays, and visual identification tasks (e.g., identifying apparatus and stating their purpose) can be included. These types of questions do not typically appear on the official CSEC Chemistry examination but are useful for deepening understanding. In-class activities and homework assignments offer the greatest flexibility for incorporating diverse assessment types.

Samples of Multiple-Choice Questions

1. Elements in the modern periodic table are arranged in order of increasing:
   a. Chemical reactivity
   b. Atomic number
   c. Mass number
   d. Relative atomic mass
2. The symbol Si stands for what element?
   a. Silicon
   b. Silver
   c. Copper
   d. Tin
3. What is the symbol for Argon?
   a. A
   b. An
   c. Ag
   d. Ar
4. What is the atomic number for beryllium?
   a. 83
   b. 4
   c. 35
   d. 5
5. Which of the following is the electronic configuration of fluorine?
   a. 2.8.8.1
   b. 2.8.1
   c. 2.8
   d. 2.7
6. What mass of oxygen contains the same number of moles as 112 g of sulfur? (RAM: O = 16; S = 32)
   a. 0.56 g
   b. 5.60 g
   c. 56.00 g
   d. 560.00 g
7. The major natural sources of alkanes and alkenes are:

a. Petroleum
b. Natural gas
c. Coal
d. The Earth's crust

8. Which of the following aqueous solutions contains 1 mole of hydrogen ions?

a. 1 dm^3 of 1.0 mol dm^{-3} H_2SO_4
b. 1 dm^3 of 1 mol dm^{-3} H_3PO_4
c. 2 dm^3 of 0.5 mol dm^{-3} H_2SO_4
d. 2 dm^3 of 0.5 mol dm^{-3} HCl

9. Which term BEST describes strong acids?

a. Fully ionized
b. Partially ionized
c. Ionized to a large extent
d. Concentrated and partially ionized

10. How much charge, in coulombs, passes through an electrolyte when a current of 100 A flows for 10 minutes?

a. 100 C
b. 600 C
c. 1,000 C
d. 60,000 C

Sample of Structure Question

A. This question is concerned with the mole and its application.

i. Give a definition for the term 'mole'.

____

____

(1 mark)

ii. Write Avogadro's constant or number.

____

____

(1 mark)

iii. Calculate the molar mass of calcium hydrogencarbonate and oxygen gas. The chemical formula for calcium hydrogencarbonate is $Ca(HCO_3)_2$, and oxygen gas is O_2.

____

____

(2 marks)

B. Calcium hydrogencarbonate reacts with nitric acid according to the following equation: $Ca(HCO_3)2(s) + 2HCl(aq) \rightarrow CaCl_2(aq) + 2CO_2(g) + 2H_2O(l)$

During an investigation in the laboratory, a student added 7.5 g of calcium hydrogencarbonate to excess hydrochloric acid.

i. Calculate the number of moles of calcium hydrogencarbonate used by the student.

____

____

(2 marks)

ii. Determine the number of moles of carbon dioxide made.

____

____

(2 marks)

iii. Calculate the volume of carbon dioxide made at r.t.p.

____

____

(2 marks)

C. A chemical bond is an attraction between atoms that holds them together.

i. Name the three main chemical bonds.

____

____

(2 mark)

ii. Using a dot-and-cross diagram, show the bonding in sodium chloride.

Na atomic number = 11 and Cl atomic number = 17.

(3 marks)

Total 15 marks

Analysis of Mid-term Test and Final Exam

Mid-term (Six-Week) Test Analysis

The six-week tests across Grades 10 and 11 primarily include 20 multiple-choice questions (Section A) and two structured questions (Section B). These test formats are intentionally modeled after the CSEC Chemistry exam to reinforce students' familiarity with national assessment standards. However, the content focus is limited to selected topics taught up to the midterm, such as states of matter, osmosis, mixtures, metals, and green chemistry. This topic-specific approach supports continuous assessment while keeping the test manageable within the school term.

Pedagogically, the inclusion of both item types (MCQs and structured responses) caters to diverse learning styles, supporting read/write learners through written responses and logical learners through process-based questioning. However, some areas need improvement. For instance, while the questions are mostly well-structured, some can include diagrams or data interpretation to increase the challenge level and enhance visual learning. Additionally, although working must be shown in Section B, more guided instructions or mark allocations per sub-question can improve clarity. To boost engagement and cognitive depth, future tests can benefit from scaffolded reasoning questions, problem-solving based on experimental scenarios, and more integration of data or case-based items that mimic SBA-style tasks. Alternative question types, such as puzzles, matching, fill-in-the-blank, short essays, and labelling diagrams, can also be considered to enrich assessment diversity.

Final Examination Analysis – Paper 1 (Multiple Choice)

Paper 1 follows the standard CSEC Chemistry multiple-choice format, comprising 60 questions covering a wide range of topics. The questions require factual recall, conceptual understanding, and basic calculation skills. The test format encourages breadth of coverage, offering students exposure to numerous topics, including atomic structure, mole calculations, bonding, electrolysis, acids and bases, and organic chemistry. The use of distractors (plausible incorrect options) is well applied in many questions, testing students' critical thinking and their ability to eliminate incorrect reasoning.

While the exam aligns closely with the CSEC format, improvements can be made by increasing the inclusion of data-based questions and visual items, such as labeled diagrams and graph interpretation, which are also featured on the official paper. Ensuring that each question targets a specific cognitive level (e.g., knowledge, application, or analysis) will enhance the diagnostic value of the assessment. As this paper mirrors the official Paper 1, it avoids alternative formats like fill-in-the-blank or matching types. This consistency helps students become familiar with and confident in handling external examination conditions.

Final Examination Analysis – Paper 2 (Structured Responses)

Paper 2 follows the CSEC Chemistry structured response format, covering essential competencies such as balanced equations, practical lab analysis, calculations, and theoretical explanations. The questions encourage clarity, critical thinking, and proper problem-solving strategies. Mark allocations are generally appropriate and support guided answering. Practical-based questions, such as those on titration and electrolysis, connect to SBA and facilitate scientific reasoning.

Since the final exam must simulate the official CSEC exam, the structure avoids alternative formats like fill-in-the-blank or a full essay (single massive essay), which are not used by the examination body. This adherence supports student familiarity with external assessment conditions. The SBA should be used to support students' preparation for exams and tests, not the other way around, by reinforcing experimental procedures, analytical writing, and lab-based reasoning in ways that align with what is expected in Paper 2.

Practical Activities

In this book, practical activities were not a major emphasis; the focus was on improving lesson delivery and supporting resources rather than developing new practicals. For CSEC Chemistry, the existing practical work is structured so that activities are reviewed before students conduct the experiments, with the teacher providing clear guidance throughout. Notes for each CSEC topic, quizzes, and instructional videos via Google Classroom are made available to prepare students in advance. These varied resources support different learning styles, such as visual and auditory. Also, learning theories like constructivism, which emphasize building understanding before practical application, are supported.

The teacher marks the completed practical work and provides written feedback for corrections, ensuring students have the opportunity to improve their work. While this feedback process strengthens learning, a key weakness is that only a small number of students consistently complete and submit laboratory reports. Also, only a few students use the videos, notes, and quizzes provided. This limited uptake impacts the quality of preparation and can delay the marking of lab reports.

Samples of Practical Activity

Organic Chemistry: Unsaturated and Saturated Compounds Experiment

Date:

Topic: Organic Chemistry-Alkanes and Alkenes

Skill: Analysis and Interpretation (AI) and Observation, Recording, and Reporting (ORR)

Theory: Make short notes on alkanes and alkenes

Aim: To investigate the effect of aqueous bromine on cyclohexane and cyclohexene.

Apparatus, materials, and reagents: Identify all apparatus, materials, and reagents by reading the method.

Method:

1. Pour 2 cm3 of cyclohexane into a test tube.
2. Pour 2cm3 of cyclohexene into another test tube.
3. Place 3 drops of bromine solution in each test tube.
4. Record all observations made.

Observation:

Discussion:

1. Why is cyclohexene considered unsaturated, while cyclohexane is considered saturated?
2. Apart from bromine, what other reagent could be used to test for saturation?
3. Write a balanced equation for the reaction between cyclohexene and bromine.
4. Write a balanced equation (which includes the conditions) for the reaction between cyclohexane and bromine.

Conclusion: *Be concise*

Unsaturated and Saturated Compounds Experiment Rubric for *ORR*		
	Criteria	Marks
A	Format: Proper lab structure	2
B	Method: Logical, past tense, accurate steps	2
C	• Observations • Colour of cyclohexane, cyclohexene and bromine • Colour change: cyclohexene and bromine • Colour change: cyclohexane and bromine	4

Unsaturated and Saturated Compounds Experiment Rubric for *ORR*		
Criteria		Marks
D	• Clear and concise report writing • Report presents the experiment properly	2
		10

Chapter 4

Review of the Data Analysis Procedure

This chapter provides a review of the data analysis procedures used to examine lesson plans, assessments, diagrams, and examinations. The purpose is to offer educators and researchers a clear, practical approach to conducting research, particularly in school settings and organizations that generate substantial documentation. Such data, when properly analyzed, can reveal underlying issues affecting institutional performance and uncover potential solutions to improve teaching, learning, and organizational outcomes.

Data Analysis Procedure

This chapter outlines the data analysis procedure used to examine instructional documents and classroom reflections with the goal of identifying pedagogical strengths, gaps, and opportunities for instructional improvement. The analysis was AI-guided and focused on lesson plans, class evaluations, hand-drawn diagrams, PowerPoint notes, mid-term tests, and final examinations. This process should serve as a model for teachers and researchers conducting research using available school documentation. The method is particularly valuable in contexts where data is abundant but underutilized, such as schools with years of lesson notes, assessments, and feedback.

Frameworks for Analysis

- Document analysis (READ Approach)
- Reflective-practitioner inquiry

Document Analysis (READ Approach)

Adapted from Bowen (2009), the READ model was used as the primary structure for analyzing textual data:

- Ready your materials: Relevant instructional materials, including class evaluations, lesson plans, homework, and classroom activities, were collected.
- Extract data: Each document was reviewed and annotated to record teaching strategies, student behaviors, instructional outcomes, and assessment methods.
- Analyze data: Documents were examined for alignment with learning theories (constructivism, behaviorism, cognitivism), learning styles (visual, auditory, kinesthetic), and instructional pacing. Strengths and weaknesses were identified.
- Distill findings: Key insights were summarized and used to develop conclusions about instructional effectiveness and areas for improvement.

Reflective-Practitioner Inquiry

Based on Schön's (1983) model, the reflective-practitioner component involved:

- Observation: Reading teacher-written evaluations and planning documents to understand real classroom contexts.
- Reflection-in-action: Considering how classroom events reflect pedagogical theory and decision-making in the moment.
- Reflection-on-action: Analyzing documents after the fact to evaluate teacher choices, instructional impact, and student outcomes.

Step 1: Document Collection and Categorization

The process began by organizing the data into four primary categories:

- Lesson Plans

- Assessment Instruments (Six-week/mid-term tests and final exams)
- Instructional Notes and Diagrams
- Class Reflections and Evaluations

Each category was reviewed independently to maintain thematic coherence and ensure that patterns could be identified based on document type.

Step 2: Lesson Plan Analysis

Lesson plans were analyzed section-by-section: objectives, 5E structure, assessment, real-world links, learning theories, and learning styles. Improvements were noted directly within the documents to preserve their original structure while enhancing clarity and alignment with the CSEC Chemistry syllabus. Each plan was assessed for how effectively it integrated:

- Learning Theories: Constructivism (student participation and knowledge construction), cognitive theory (scaffolded instruction and cognitive chunking), and behaviorism (reinforcement via quizzes and feedback).
- Learning Styles: Visual (diagrams, charts), auditory (oral presentations, discussions), kinesthetic (labs, hands-on demos), and read/write (notes, worksheets).

Real-world applications (e.g., calculating rum concentration or interpreting food labels) were noted as powerful anchors for engagement. Opportunities for improvement included more varied engagement activities, explicit connections to national development, and enhanced integration with other science subjects such as Biology and Physics.

Step 3: Assessment Instrument Review

Assessment documents, including six-week tests, mid-term papers, and final exams, were evaluated for content coverage, structure, and variety. Tests were grouped by type (e.g., multiple-choice, structured response, calculation-based), and each question was coded according to the cognitive demand (recall, application, analysis).

- Mid-Term Tests had most items designed to mirror the CSEC format, aligning with the expectation for external exam preparation. However, diversification is possible using a variety of question types.
- Final Exams (mock exams and end-of-term tests) were highly structured to resemble official CSEC Chemistry papers. These included Paper 1 (multiple-choice) and Paper 2 (structured responses). Due to the need for external alignment, formats such as fill-in-the-blank or true/false were avoided. Item analysis suggested strong alignment with key syllabus topics, but opportunities to include more problem-based and case-analysis questions were identified.

Step 4: Instructional Notes and Diagrams

Class diagrams and PowerPoints were reviewed for scientific accuracy, clarity, and instructional value. Visuals were primarily hand-drawn in class due to limited access to projectors or smartboards, but they remained highly effective.

Three sample diagrams on crystallization were analyzed to determine:

- Labeling accuracy
- Completeness of visual stages
- Explanatory depth

These diagrams supported visual learning, reinforced mental models, and served as cognitive anchors. Recommendations included adding flow arrows, writing titles for diagrams and charts, and pairing images with short explanations. PowerPoint notes also incorporated YouTube links for extended learning and were clear and relevant to the syllabus.

Step 5: Reflection and Evaluation Review

Teacher reflections and student feedback were read and thematically coded using recurring terms like clarity, engagement, discipline challenges, and comprehension issues. Patterns in student misunderstanding, identified through the educator's analysis of instructional materials (e.g., mole calculations or titration analysis), can inform improvements in lesson planning by:

- Adding scaffolded mole problems with partial answers
- Using substances (sugar, salt, etc.) in class for concentration calculations
- Labeling apparatus for titration

These insights ensured that teaching and learning were grounded in classroom realities rather than just theory.

Step 6: Coding and Thematic Grouping

A simple coding matrix was used to track features across documents:

Code	Description	Document Type
LT	Learning Theory Applied	Lesson Plans, Notes
LS	Learning Style Addressed	All Materials
RW	Real-World Application Included	Lesson Plans, Diagrams
AA	Assessment Aligned with CSEC Format	Tests, Exams
VR	Visual Representation (e.g., diagrams)	Diagrams, PowerPoints
FF	Feedback from Reflection Used	Class Evaluations

Table 5.1

This simple matrix allowed the researcher to match classroom practices with curriculum requirements and pedagogical best practices.

Raw Excerpt	Code	Category	Grouped Theme
"Grade 10A behavior still not	Disruptive behavior	Classroom Management	Behavioral Challenges

Raw Excerpt	Code	Category	Grouped Theme
acceptable"			
"Students completed filtration lab"	Lab activity	Assessment Type	Practical Learning
"Used drawing of atomic model"	Visual aid	Learning Style	Visual Engagement
"Topic completed in two weeks"	Timely coverage	Pacing	Instructional Alignment
"Used article review and discussion"	Critical thinking	Learning Theory	Constructivist Strategy

Table 5.2

Step 7: Reflective Synthesis and Instructional Feedback

Following the analysis, notes were compiled to recommend how instructional practices could improve:

- More use of scaffolded exercises
- More visible real-world ties (via labels, packaging, beverages)
- Clearer assessment rubrics and guided sub-questions
- Use of mobile platforms (e.g., WhatsApp) to supplement audio-visual learning sharing when smartboards and projectors are unavailable

The AI-guided data analysis procedure presented here is practical and replicable. It shows how existing instructional material, when systematically reviewed, can reveal gaps, confirm strengths, and guide instructional reform. This strategy promotes data-driven teaching, improves CSEC Chemistry preparation, and supports classroom-based research. Educators across varying contexts can adopt this method to enhance both daily instruction and long-term student outcomes.

Chapter 5
Discussion

This book aimed to develop a reflective chemistry education resource informed by real classroom materials and aligned with sound teaching practices. The review of literature revealed eleven components of chemistry education proposed by the researcher: conceptual learning and modeling, misconceptions and threshold concepts, laboratory skills development, cognitive load in practical work, assessment and feedback, curriculum structure and progression, technology integration, societal and real-world contexts, student motivation and engagement, inclusivity and differentiation, and communication and scientific literacy. Those eleven elements were reflected in the analysis of the educational materials and in the improvements proposed by the book. Conceptual learning and modeling involve helping students mentally organize chemical ideas. This was demonstrated through activities such as writing balanced equations, classifying chemical reactions, and identifying mole ratios from chemical formulas. Misconceptions and threshold concepts refer to common misunderstandings or difficult concepts that can block progress. One worksheet addressed this by having students define and differentiate between ions and molecules, with teacher comments guiding conceptual correction.

Laboratory skills development refers to students' ability to perform practical experiments correctly and confidently. In this book, students would carry out activities such as weighing substances, preparing standard solutions, and using burettes to perform titrations. Cognitive load in practical work involves organizing tasks to prevent students from being overwhelmed. The teacher used labeled diagrams and sequenced instructions to support student focus during experiments. Assessment and feedback are essential for tracking progress and addressing learning gaps. Examples included drawing tasks, one-minute reflections, and exit tickets, all of which were used to gather student responses and provide feedback for improvement.

Curriculum structure and progression refer to the logical order in which topics are taught. The teacher introduced basic concepts, such as chemical names and formulas, before progressing to mole calculations and solution preparation, allowing students to build knowledge step by step. Technology integration involves using digital tools to enhance learning. YouTube videos were used to reinforce lessons on molecular structure and solution preparation, providing visual support and extended explanation. Societal and real-world contexts relate chemistry to students' everyday lives. The teacher can use food packaging labels to teach mole calculations and alcoholic beverages to illustrate concentration, making abstract content more relatable.

Student motivation and engagement refer to how actively students participate in lessons. In this case, students were asked to deliver brief oral summaries, complete drawing tasks, and handle lab equipment, which maintained interest and promoted involvement. Inclusivity and differentiation involve meeting the diverse needs of students. This was achieved by using multiple activity formats, such as fill-in-the-blank tasks, drawing exercises, and step-by-step lab instructions, which allowed students with different learning preferences to participate. Communication and scientific literacy mean the ability to express and understand scientific information accurately. Students were required to label diagrams, define chemical terms, and write planning and design sections, all of which helped them communicate chemistry using proper structure and vocabulary.

These findings indicate that the teacher practiced sound pedagogy grounded in reflection and theory. The materials provided clear opportunities for students to interact with content, practice essential skills, and express their understanding through multiple formats. The learning approaches applied included constructivism, the 5E model, and experiential learning, each supported by real classroom examples. Constructivist strategies were evident in guided inquiry worksheets, while the 5E model was reflected in the lesson structures that included engagement, exploration, explanation, elaboration and evaluation. Learning styles were addressed by including visual tasks (e.g., drawing), kinesthetic tasks (e.g., lab activities), and reflective writing tasks (e.g., one-minute reflection papers). These instructional approaches showed the teacher's effort to connect theory to classroom practice.

The main strengths observed in the classroom materials include detailed lesson planning, structured lab activities, and consistent evaluation tools. Each lesson plan included measurable objectives, appropriate content coverage, and differentiated activities such as drawing diagrams, conducting group work, and solving mole calculations. Practical worksheets were used to help students practice real-world chemistry skills, such as titration and solution preparation. Student engagement was promoted through oral presentations, drawing tasks, and calculation-based problems. These approaches aligned with good teaching practice and showed evidence of thoughtful design across multiple lessons.

Despite the overall strength of the materials, some weaknesses were identified that can guide improvement. In several lessons, reflection or evaluation sections were either missing or underdeveloped, reducing opportunities for teacher feedback and student self-assessment. In certain lab activities, the evaluation criteria were not clearly outlined, and student instructions were either incomplete or overly general. An incomplete instruction is "stop titration when a faint pink color appears," which fails to state that the color must persist for 30 seconds, whereas the correct instruction is "using phenolphthalein add the titrant dropwise and stop when a faint pink persists for 30 seconds." While a general instruction is "wash your hands after each experiment." This can cause teachers to overlook advising students to also wash their faces after certain experiments, especially since students might unknowingly touch their faces.

Additionally, while multiple learning styles were addressed through a variety of tasks, more direct use of tools such as differentiated rubrics or tiered questions could further support diverse learners. The reflection sheets also revealed that some objectives were not always met due to limited time or incomplete follow-through. These areas suggest that with small adjustments, the resource can be strengthened further to support deeper understanding and inclusivity.

Teacher reflection played a central role in the development and revision of the instructional materials. Each evaluation form was used to identify what worked and what needed improvement, showing a deliberate attempt to refine pedagogy. For example, the teacher noted when students were confused by the wording of a homework question and rewrote it for future use. In other cases, lesson objectives were adjusted to focus more clearly on key concepts such as mole-to-mass conversions or acid-base neutralization. These reflections supported a cycle of continuous improvement and provided a strong foundation for teacher professional growth.

The classroom evaluations also revealed how the teacher's use of management strategies impacted learning. Lessons included assigned roles during lab sessions, reminders for safety, and clear classroom rules to maintain order. Students were grouped purposefully for collaboration and were held accountable for participation through group work and practical tasks. These structures created a predictable learning environment where students could engage meaningfully without disruption. The teacher's consistent use of management tools contributed to an efficient lesson flow and gave students confidence in their tasks.

Compared to findings in the literature review, the classroom practices were mostly aligned with international expectations for scientific teaching. The use of inquiry-based activities, varied assessments, and practical applications supported the idea that meaningful learning happens when students interact directly with the content. The application of the 5E model, the use of VARK strategies, and the incorporation of constructivist principles reflect best practices supported by educational research. In some areas, such as differentiated instruction or extensive technology use, the practices can be extended further. However, the reflective nature of the teaching indicates readiness for such growth.

The material also showed strong alignment between theory and real-world classroom use. Chemistry topics were introduced through accessible examples like cooking, cleaning, and consumer products. It is proposed that students will calculate the moles of salt to be used for tasks such as cooking, explore alcohol percentages in drinks to determine concentration, and interpret nutritional labels, all of which will link academic content to life outside school. These approaches not only support conceptual understanding but also make lessons more meaningful and memorable for students. This connection between theory and practical relevance is essential for long-term retention and engagement.

This book demonstrates that a well-structured, reflective resource based on real classroom practice can benefit chemistry teachers across various settings. The examples provided are practical, clear, and aligned with both learning theories and examination standards. Teachers can use this resource to guide their own lesson planning, cater to multiple learning styles, assess student understanding, and reflect on their instructional methods. The findings suggest that this resource, once revised in response to suggestions, can serve as a practical guidebook for chemistry and general science educators seeking to improve student learning through structured, theory-based pedagogy.

Conclusion

This book was motivated by long-standing challenges in the teaching and learning of CSEC Chemistry, including difficulties in syllabus completion, conceptual understanding, and student engagement. To address these concerns, the book utilized classroom materials such as lesson plans, assessments, evaluations, and teacher reflections that had already been implemented in real teaching contexts. These materials were analyzed to identify instructional strengths and weaknesses and to propose improvements grounded in reflective practice and educational theory.

The purpose of the research was to explore how a teacher-developed chemistry education resource, informed by learning theories and learning styles, could improve instructional quality. The findings affirm that aligning teaching practices with theoretical frameworks and learner preferences enhances clarity, engagement, and inclusivity in science instruction.

A central contribution of this thesis is the articulation of 11 components of chemistry education: conceptual learning and modeling, misconceptions and threshold concepts, laboratory skills development, cognitive load in practical work, assessment and feedback, curriculum structure and progression, technology integration, societal and real-world contexts, student motivation and engagement, inclusivity and differentiation, and communication and scientific literacy. These components emerged from a rigorous literature review and are presented as new knowledge to guide instructional development in secondary chemistry education.

The book also highlights the importance of applying learning theories, such as constructivism, cognitive load theory, and social learning theory, alongside learning styles, including visual, auditory, and kinesthetic modalities. These frameworks helped transform content delivery into more differentiated, accessible, and cognitively balanced instruction. Their use not only enhanced student participation and understanding but also provided teachers with actionable strategies to address varied learner needs.

Additionally, the analysis underscored the importance of effective behavior management strategies in creating a productive learning environment. Approaches such as establishing clear classroom rules, reinforcing positive behaviors, and employing consistent consequences were identified as essential for maintaining order and supporting academic focus. Strategies such as active supervision, structured group work, and proactive engagement techniques can minimize disruptions while fostering mutual respect between teachers and students. Integrating these practices with instructional improvements ensures that the classroom climate remains conducive to learning, thereby supporting the overall success of the proposed chemistry education resource.

The outcomes of this thesis hold meaningful benefits for multiple stakeholders. For teachers, the resource offers practical, evidence-based strategies that are adaptable to diverse classroom contexts, enabling them to enhance both lesson delivery and student engagement. For researchers, it contributes a structured framework of 11 components that can serve as a foundation for future studies in chemistry education, reflective practice, and instructional design. For society, improved science education fosters a better-prepared student population with critical thinking, scientific literacy, and problem-solving skills essential for addressing real-world challenges. By bridging theory, practice, and societal needs, the book reinforces the role of education as a driver of personal and community advancement.

In sum, this research contributes to the growing body of evidence supporting reflective, theory-informed teaching. It emphasizes that even modest classroom data, when systematically analyzed, can yield powerful insights for instructional reform.

References

1. American Chemical Society. (n.d.). *Technology in the classroom.* American Chemical Society. Retrieved July 27, 2025, from https://www.acs.org/education/policies/middle-and-high-school-chemistry/classroom/technology.html
2. American Chemical Society International Historic Chemical Landmarks. (n.d.). *Antoine Laurent Lavoisier: The Chemical Revolution.* American Chemical Society. Retrieved July 11, 2025, from https://www.acs.org/education/whatischemistry/landmarks/lavoisier.html
3. Amr, S. S., & Tbakhi, A. (2007). Jabir ibn Hayyan. *Annals of Saudi Medicine, 27*(1), 52–53. https://doi.org/10.5144/0256-4947.2007.53
4. Azize, J. (2023). The Emerald Tablet in Arabic, Latin, and English. *Lucida: Journal of the Australasian Association of Philosophy, 1*(1), 1–21. https://doi.org/10.16953/lucida.21007
5. Bada, S. O. (2015). Constructivism learning theory: A paradigm for teaching and learning. *IOSR Journal of Research & Method in Education (IOSR JRME), 5*(6, Version I), 66–70. https://doi.org/10.9790/7388 05616670
6. Banerjee, A. (2004). Colonialism and its educational legacy: The British case. *Journal of Social History, 37*(4), 1011–1033.
7. Barke, H.-D., Hazari, A., & Yitbarek, S. (2009). *Misconceptions in chemistry: Addressing perceptions in chemical education.* Springer.
8. Berman, T. (1983). The University of Paris: Its origins and development. *Higher Education Journal, 5*(2), 177–191.

9. Black, P., & Wiliam, D. (2009). Developing the theory of formative assessment. *Educational Assessment, Evaluation and Accountability, 21*(1), 5–31.
10. Brush, S. G., Spencer, J. B., & Osler, M. J. (2025, February 13). Scientific Revolution. *Encyclopedia Britannica.* https://www.britannica.com/science/Scientific Revolution
11. California Department of Education. (n.d.). *Assessment, evaluation, and reporting.* https://www.cde.ca.gov/ci/gs/ps/evalrept.asp
12. Cavallo, G. (2001). The University of Bologna: A historical overview. *European History Quarterly, 16*(1), 23–45.
13. Çelikler, D. (2020). A comparison of the learning styles of chemistry students and chemistry education students in universities in Turkey. *African Educational Research Journal, 8*(4), 841–848. https://files.eric.ed.gov/fulltext/EJ1274225.pdf
14. Center for Comprehensive School Reform and Improvement. (2009, August 15). *Vertical alignment: Ensuring opportunity to learn in a standards-based system* (Issue Brief, ED507587). US Department of Education. https://files.eric.ed.gov/fulltext/ED507587.pdf
15. Cornell University Center for Teaching Innovation. (n.d.). *Rubrics.* https://teaching.cornell.edu/teaching-resources/assessment-evaluation/rubrics
16. Coyne, G. L. (2023, January 15). Lead to Gold, Sorcery to Science: Alchemy and the Foundations of Modern Chemistry. *PIT Journal.* https://pitjournal.unc.edu/2023/01/15/lead-to-gold-sorcery-to-science-alchemy-and-the-foundations-of-modern-chemistry/
17. CXC. (n.d.-a). *About CXC: Mission and Vision.* Caribbean Examinations Council. Retrieved July 15, 2025, from https://www.cxc.org/about/about-cxc/

18. CXC. (n.d.-b). *History of CXC.* Caribbean Examinations Council. Retrieved July 15, 2025, from https: //www.cxc.org/about history/
19. CXC. (n.d.-c). *Background.* Caribbean Examinations Council. Retrieved July 15, 2025, from https: // www.cxc.org/about background/
20. Darling-Hammond, L., & Adamson, F. (2014). *Beyond the bubble test: How performance assessments support 21st century learning.* John Wiley & Sons.
21. Davis, D. J. (2022, March 15). History highlights the bond between science and religion. *Houston Christian University.* https://hc.edu/news-and-events/2022/03/15/history-highlights-the-bond-between-science-and-religion/
22. Davis, M. L., Witcraft, S. M., Baird, S. O., & Smits, J. A. J. (2017). Learning principles in CBT. In S. G. Hofmann & G. J. Asmundson (Eds.), *The science of cognitive behavioral therapy* (pp. 51–76). Academic Press. https://doi.org/10.1016/B978-0-12-803457-6.00003-9
23. De Vries, J. (2002). The guild system in medieval Europe. *Economic History Review, 49*(3), 547–567.
24. Deboer, G. E. (1991). *A history of ideas in science education: Implications for practice.* Teachers College Press.
25. *Experiential learning.* (2021). Institute for Teaching and Learning Innovation, University of Queensland. Retrieved July 25, 2025, from https://itali.uq.edu.au/teaching-guidance/teaching-practices/active-learning/experiential-learning
26. Field, M. (2016). The fall of New Hampshire State College: A historical analysis. *History of Education Quarterly, 56*(2), 205–222.
27. GCU Blog. (2024, July 11). *10 positive classroom management strategies.* Grand Canyon University. Retrieved July 31, 2025, from https://www.gcu.edu/blog/teaching-school-administration/positive-classroom-management-strategies

28. Ghaicha, A. (2016). Theoretical framework for educational assessment: A synoptic review. *Journal of Education and Practice, 7*(24), 212–231.
29. Green, P. (2003). Education and war: Post-World War I educational reforms. *Journal of Global Education, 17*(4), 243–257.
30. Hofstein, A., & Lunetta, V. N. (2004). The laboratory in science education: Foundations for the twenty-first century. *Science Education, 88*(1), 28–54.
31. Hutchins, J. A. (2020). Tailoring scientific communications for the audience and the research narrative. *Current Protocols Essential Laboratory Techniques, 20*(1), e40. https://doi.org/10.1002/cpet.40
32. Ignatik, K. (n.d.). *A history of the Scientific Revolution.* Hillsdale College. Retrieved July 10, 2025, from https://www.hillsdale.edu/hillsdale-blog/k12-classical-education/a-history-of-the-scientific-revolution/
33. Jackson, P. W. (1992). *Life in Classrooms.* Teachers College Press.
34. Jamaica Information Service. (2024a, August 20). *Jamaican students performed marginally higher in the 2024 CSEC mathematics exam.* https://jis.gov.jm/jamaican-students-perform-marginally-higher-in-2024-csec-mathematics-exam/
35. Jamaica Information Service. (2024b, August 26). *CAPE students maintain a high level of performance.* https://jis.gov.jm/cape-students-maintain-high-level-of-performance/
36. Jamaica Teachers' Association. (2025, March 28). *Jamaica's education system: A call to action.* https://www.jta.org.jm/content/jamaica-launches-go-public-fund-education-campaign-amid-critical-teacher-shortage

37. Johnstone, A. H., & Al-Shuaili, A. (2001). Learning in the laboratory: Some thoughts from the literature. *University Chemistry Education, 5*(2), 42–51.
38. Kaieteur News. (2024, August 21). *Caribbean-wide decline in CSEC, CAPE passes.* https://www.kaieteurnewsonline.com/2024/08/21/caribbean-wide-decline-in-csec-cape-passes/
39. Katz, M. (1987). Horace Mann and the origins of American education. *History of Education Quarterly, 27*(2), 143–167.
40. Killen, R. (2016). *Effective teaching strategies: Lessons from research and practice* (7th ed.). Cengage Learning.
41. King, D. (2012). New perspectives on context-based chemistry education. *Studies in Science Education, 48*(1), 51–87.
42. Knight, D. (1992). *Ideas in chemistry: A history of the science.* Rutgers University Press.
43. Kousa, P., & Aksela, M. (2019). Promoting students' interest and learning in chemistry through culturally responsive teaching. *LUMAT, 7*(1), 68–91.
44. Kramer, D. (2015). The New England War on Satan and its educational implications. *Religious History Review, 22*(3), 58–72.
45. Kumar, A. (2022). Teaching methods, strategies, techniques, and approaches. *International Journal of Advanced Research in Science, Communication and Technology, 2*(2).
46. Larson, E. (2020). The history of chemistry: Chemical education in the United States. *The Synapse: Intercollegiate Science Magazine, 22*(1), Article 10.
47. Leong, E., Mercer, A., Danczak, S. M., Kyne, S. H., & Thompson, C. D. (2021). The transition to first-year chemistry. *Chemistry Education Research and Practice, 22*(4), 793–808.
48. Litt, D. (2007). The role of female teachers in 19th-century education. *Women in Education, 6*(1), 35–48.

49. Machost, H., & Stains, M. (2023). Reflective practices in education. *CBE Life Sciences Education, 22*, es2.
50. Mamoon-Al-Bashir, A., Kabir, R., & Rahman, I. (2016). The value and effectiveness of feedback. *Journal of Education and Practice, 7*(16), 38–41.
51. Martínez-Arboleda, A. (2021). Using ipsative assessment for reflective learning. *Journal of University Teaching & Learning Practice, 18*(3), 66–82.
52. Moseley, R. (2001). Ida Freund: Her life and contribution to science education. *Education in Chemistry, 38*(3), 76–78.
53. National Research Council. (2021). *Innovations in teaching science: A 21st-century approach.* National Academies Press.
54. National Research Council (US) Committee on Challenges in Chemistry Graduate Education. (2012). *Challenges in chemistry graduate education: A workshop summary.* National Academies Press.
55. Nielsen, K. (2010). Apprenticeship approach to learning. In P. Peterson et al. (Eds.), *International encyclopedia of education* (3rd ed.). Elsevier.
56. Northern Illinois University Center for Innovative Teaching and Learning. (2012). *Formative and summative assessment.*
57. Office of Educational Improvement, Medical College of Wisconsin. (2022, May). *Cognitive load theory: A guide to applying cognitive load theory to your teaching.*
58. OECD. (2022). *Teachers and leaders in schools: Preparing for the future.* OECD Publishing.
59. Organization for Economic Co-operation and Development. (n.d.-b). *Teacher professional learning and development.* OECD.
60. Oye, N. D. (2001). History of the pedagogical reform movement. In *International encyclopedia of the social & behavioral sciences.*
61. Price, W. S., & Hill, J. O. (2004). Raising the status of chemistry education. *University Chemistry Education, 8*, 13–17.

62. Renn, J., & Damerow, P. (2015). Scientific Revolution, history and sociology of. In *International encyclopedia of the social & behavioral sciences.*
63. Robinson, A. (2002). The invention of writing and its impact on education. *Ancient Civilizations Journal, 14*(3), 102–120.
64. Royal Society of Chemistry. (n.d.). *Aqua regia.* Royal Society of Chemistry.
65. Ryan, R. M., & Deci, E. L. (2000). Intrinsic and extrinsic motivations. *Contemporary Educational Psychology, 25*(1), 54–67.
66. SAGE Publications. (n.d.). *Evaluation.* In *SAGE Research Methods.*
67. Schön, D. A. (1983). *The reflective practitioner.* Basic Books.
68. Shandomo, H. M. (2009). The role of critical reflection in teacher education. *School–University Partnerships, 4*(1), 101–113.
69. Sherma, A. B. (2023). Perfectionist process and adaptability in EFL classrooms. *Journal of English Teaching, 9*(3), 335–349.
70. Singh Wilmot, M. (2024, August 8). *Jamaica, the 'STEM Island' – A dream that can come true.* The UWI.
71. Snyder, C. (2009). The Reformation and education. *History of Religious Education, 45*(1), 56–68.
72. Solomon, J. (2024). *A review of major violent incidents in Jamaican schools* [Master's thesis].
73. Starr, L. (2014). *Assessment and evaluation: What's the difference?* Education World.
74. Sternberg, R. J., Chowkase, A., Parra-Martinez, A., & Landy, J. (2022). Assessing student learning. *Psychology Teaching Review, 28*(2), 55–64.
75. Stojanovska, M., Mijić, I., & Petruševski, V. M. (2020). Challenges and recommendations for improving chemistry education. *CEPS Journal, 10*(1), 145–164.

76. Suits, J. P., & Sanger, M. J. (2013). Dynamic animations versus static pictures. *Chemistry Education Research and Practice, 14*(1), 65–74.
77. Sweeder, R. D., Herrington, D. G., & Crandell, O. M. (2023). Chemistry education research at a crossroads. *Journal of Chemical Education, 100*(5), 1710–1715.
78. Taber, K. S. (2013). Revisiting the chemistry triplet. *Chemistry Education Research and Practice, 14*(2), 156–168.
79. Talanquer, V. (2015). Threshold concepts in chemistry. *Journal of Chemical Education, 92*(1), 3–9.
80. Teixeira, A. C., da Silva, F. C., & de Souza, L. C. (2012). Teaching of physics and chemistry in Brazil. *arXiv.*
81. Tierney, B. (2013). Monastic schools and preserving knowledge. *Medieval Education Review, 11*(1), 1–19.
82. UNESCO (2023). Global education monitoring report: Technology in education – A tool whose terms? UNESCO Publishing.
83. University of Colorado Boulder Libraries. (n.d.). *European science before the year 1600.*
84. University of Oxford, Department of Chemistry. (n.d.). *Chemical education.*
85. University of the West Indies, Mona. (2023). *Academic portrait of students: 2020–21 to 2022–23.*
86. Villafañe, S. M., Jang, S. R., & Lewis, J. E. (2021). Addressing attrition in undergraduate chemistry. *Journal of Chemical Education, 98*(11), 3434–3443.
87. Wilkinson, F. (2024, November 15). *Industrial Revolution and technology.* National Geographic Society.
88. Wijnen-Meijer, M. (2019). Integration in the light of curriculum design. *GMS Journal for Medical Education, 36*(6).
89. Yore, L. D., Hand, B. M., & Florence, M. K. (2004). Scientists' views of science and writing practices. *Journal of Research in Science Teaching, 41*(4), 338–369.

www.ingramcontent.com/pod-product-compliance
Lightning Source LLC
Chambersburg PA
CBHW050018170726
48282CB00025B/448